Susanna Wesley:
a Radical in the
Rectory

By the same author

Shut Up Sarah (Highland Books)
Don't Call Me sister (Highland Books)
Improving Your Written English (How To Books)
Researching for Writers (How To Books)

(*For children, in collaboration with Elaine Ashmore*)
Noah's Mud and other recipes (Kevin Mayhew)

About the author

Marion Field was a school teacher for many years, but gave up her teaching career several years ago to concentrate on writing. After having many magazine articles published, she is now concentrating on book-length projects. A member of the Society of Authors, The Society of Women Writers and Journalists and the Association of Christian Writers, Marion is happy to talk to groups about her experiences. The account of her own involvement with the Exclusive Brethren is told in *Don't Call Me Sister*.

Her other interests include reading, acting and travelling. She is an active member of her local Anglican Church.

Susanna Wesley: a Radical in the Rectory

Marion Field

Highland Books

GODALMING
SURREY

First published in the UK by Highland Books 2 High Pines, Knoll Road, Godalming, Surrey, GU7 2EP

© 1998 Marion Field

All Scripture quotations, unless otherwise noted, are taken from the Authorized (or King James) Version, Crown copyright.

ISBN: 1-897913-47-8

Cover design by Martin Harris. Cover illustration by kind permission of The Methodist Church (Methodist Missionary Society Archives)

Printed in Finland by W S O Y.

ACKNOWLEDGEMENTS

I should like to thank the following people and organisations for their help in the researching and writing of this book:

- All the assistants at the Woking Library who spared no pains to search for the resource material I needed.

- Mrs Janet Henderson, the Librarian at Wesley College, Bristol, where I spent an enjoyable morning studying Susanna's Journals and letters.

- Mr C.J.Barton, the Warden at The Old Rectory, Epworth, where I was able to see where Susanna had lived.

- The Curator, Miss Noorah Al-Gailani, and her assistants at Wesley's Chapel, City Road, London. They were all very helpful and Miss Al-Gailani had removed from display one of Susanna's letters for me to photograph.

- Mrs Joy Fox, Mr John Lenton, Mr Peter Forsaith, Methodist Missionary Archives/Church and History Committee.

- Mr Christopher Webster, Tate Picture Gallery

- Mr John Basset who drew the map of Epworth and surrounding Lincolnshire.

Finally I should like to thank Mrs Stella Tassell for her help in checking the completed manuscript.

DEDICATION

To my mother who has always
given me such encouragement

Contents

A Determined Daughter *11*

An Enlightened Mother *23*

An Unpopular Rector *43*

Imprisoned For Debt! *63*

Fire At Epworth Rectory *83*

Starting Again *94*

The Rectory Ghost *110*

Whatever Happened to Susanna's Brother? *128*

Hetty Elopes *149*

Exiled To Wroot *171*

Susanna Mourns For Samuel *187*

The Widow Makes Her Mark *196*

Epilogue *210*

Bibliography *212*

PREFACE

Susanna Wesley has been a fascinating lady to research. She grew up in fairly luxurious surroundings but spent all her married life in poverty and difficulty. Her unswerving faith and serenity guided her through all her problems. In order to make the biography of this remarkable woman as readable as possible, I have incorporated some phrases taken from letters and diaries into the dialogue to recreate the atmosphere and have occasionally invented minor incidents or details which set the work firmly in its time. I hope I have avoided any anachronisms and apologise if any have crept in!

Ahead of her time in much of her thinking, Susanna was never afraid to speak her mind even if others did not agree with her. She was not a typical eighteenth century wife, dominated by her husband. Her determination that her daughters should be well-educated and her popular 'kitchen sermons' showed her indeed to be a radical in the rectory. This courage to innovate cannot have failed to impress her son John Wesley in his preaching work across England.

Marion Field
Autumn 1998

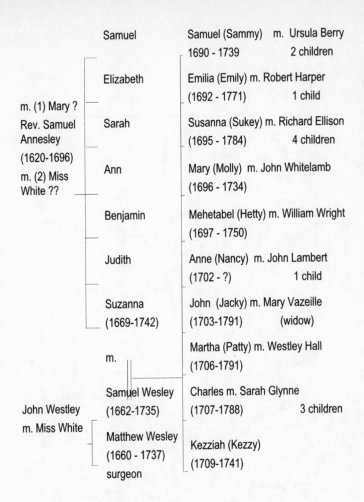

Samuel	Samuel (Sammy) m. Ursula Berry 1690 - 1739 2 children	
Elizabeth	Emilia (Emily) m. Robert Harper (1692 - 1771) 1 child	
Sarah	Susanna (Sukey) m. Richard Ellison (1695 - 1784) 4 children	
Ann	Mary (Molly) m. John Whitelamb (1696 - 1734)	
Benjamin	Mehetabel (Hetty) m. William Wright (1697 - 1750)	
Judith	Anne (Nancy) m. John Lambert (1702 - ?) 1 child	
Suzanna (1669-1742)	John (Jacky) m. Mary Vazeille (1703-1791) (widow)	

m. (1) Mary ?
Rev. Samuel Annesley (1620-1696)
m. (2) Miss White ??

m.

Samuel Wesley (1662-1735)

John Westley m. Miss White

Matthew Wesley (1660 - 1737) surgeon

Martha (Patty) m. Westley Hall (1706-1791)

Charles m. Sarah Glynne (1707-1788)   3 children

Kezziah (Kezzy) (1709-1741)

Family Tree of the Wes(t)leys and Annesleys

Many children died at birth or soon after, including nine of Susanna's. These have not been included.

Map of Epworth and surrounding Lincolnshire

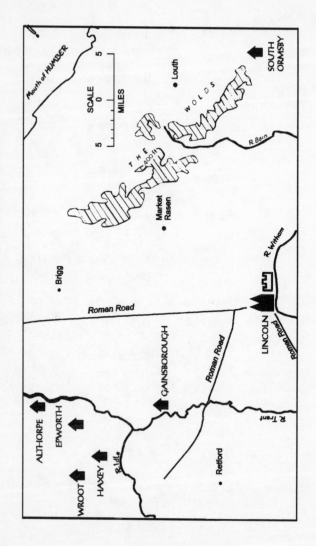

CHAPTER ONE

A Determined Daughter

"I cannot agree with you, Papa. I want to return to the Church of England."

Dr Annesley gazed sadly at his youngest daughter. Susanna was only twelve but already she was showing the independence of mind that would characterise her life. Her father was certain she would not have come to such a momentous decision without great thought and prayer. He sighed. A fair man, he had always been willing to listen to his children — an unusual characteristic in a seventeenth century father. He had been married twice; his first wife had died giving birth to their firstborn. He had married again and his second wife had produced twenty-four children — not all of whom survived. Since she too had died, Dr Annesley had to be both mother *and* father to his surviving children.[1] He knew the intelligent young daughter who now stood

---

1   Dr Annesley had obtained a degree from Queen's College Oxford in 1639 just before the start of the Civil War that

before him did not share his views about the established church so he was not surprised at her decision.

He gazed thoughtfully at her. Without doubt she was the prettiest of his five daughters although she was the most serious of them. One of her most delightful traits was her serenity in all situations and she had a 'natural piety' which endeared her to him. He also delighted in her sharp mind; by the standards of the day she was well educated. In the late twentieth century she would have had no difficulty in obtaining a good degree but that, of course, was unheard of in the seventeenth century. However, Susanna and her sisters received an education far superior to most girls of their day. They were even encouraged to take part in theological

---

plunged England into such tumult. He was sympathetic to the simple Puritan ways of worship which eschewed ritual and concentrated on the basic tenets of Christianity. They wished to abolish any ceremonies that were not based on Scripture and felt much in the Church of England needed to be reformed. Sympathetic to Puritan views, Dr Annesley was eventually ordained a Presbyterian Minister and in 1645 he became Rector of Cliffe, a wealthy Living in Kent. However, although he approved of The Puritans' ideals, he was extremely critical of Oliver Cromwell whom he regarded as a hypocrite. As he had no hesitation in saying so in public, he was removed from his lucrative living but he was eventually restored to favour and became Vicar of St Giles, Cripplegate.

When Charles II was restored to the Throne in 1660, the Church of England once again became the established Church with its Prayer Book, Bishops and set pattern of service. Dr Annesley did not wish to follow the rigid patterns of service that were now demanded of him and rather than go against his conscience, he, with many others of like mind, resigned his living. Those who objected to the Church of England in this way became known as Dissenters or Nonconformists and they suffered much persecution from the authorities.

discussions around the meal table — something at which Susanna excelled. Her upbringing left an indelible mark on her and influenced the way she was later to bring up her own children.

Dr Annesley realised his favourite daughter was still waiting for his reaction. He smiled at her. "You know, my child, that I feel much of the ritual of the Church of England is not based on the Bible. I fear the way is open for more deviations from Scripture."

"Yes, Papa, and I agree with you that it is dangerous to practise that which is not from Holy Scripture. But you have allowed me to attend Church of England services and I am grateful for that. I have found them reverent and full of meaning for me."

"You do not like the more informal services that I lead," said her father, smiling.

Susanna blushed. "Papa, I know how deeply sincere you are and I am very mindful of what you have taught me. I realise how important it is to spend some portion of the day in prayer and meditation. But I have also been impressed with the preaching of some great men in the Church of England. There is still conflict amongst Dissenters. I think, I think — " She hesitated. Was it presumptuous of her to preach to her own father who had taught her so much? But he had also instructed her to be true to her own conscience. She continued. "The Church of England seems to me a little more … secure, and—and I love the order and beauty of the services. And the Creeds that are said do not contradict the doctrine you hold, do they?"

"No, Susanna. I admit they do not." He paused before he spoke again. He was sure his daughter would not change her mind whatever he said to her. "You are determined, Susanna?"

"Yes, Papa," she whispered.

"Very well."

"Oh thank you, Papa." Susanna clasped her hands together and beamed at him. Then she frowned. "You don't mind too much, do you?"

He smiled. "I'm sorry you feel as you do, Susanna, but I know you are sincere and I respect your views."

"You are the best Papa anyone could have."

"Thank you, my dear. Let us pray before you go."

Susanna knelt by the chair and bowed her head as her father prayed for a blessing on his favourite daughter. When he had finished, she stood up and dropping a curtsey, she hurried through the door beaming with satisfaction and relief. She loved her father and he would always exert a great influence on her although she disagreed with some of his views. Her simple Puritan upbringing, in spite of her love for the more flamboyant Church of England, was deeply ingrained in her and she never forgot what her father had taught her. Many of the Puritan values, which had been instilled in her, she later passed on to her own children.

She kept a journal in which she recorded her thoughts. Intelligent and thoughtful, she appreciated the regular family prayers, Bible readings and instruction in the Christian faith she received from her father. However she wrote in her journal that she often became 'discouraged by the experience of daily renewed failings'. To attempt to counteract this she determined 'never to spend more time in mere recreation in one day than I spend in private religious devotions'[2]. Throughout her life, in spite of difficulties she tried to maintain this high standard.

---

2   G.J.Stevenson, *Memorials of the Wesley Family*

Life was hazardous at the end of the seventeenth century with fire risk from open fires and candles and the possibility of accidents when travelling by horse on the roads or boat on the river. Like many of her contemporaries, Susanna escaped death on several occasions and wrote in her journal of her 'preservation from ill accidents and once from a violent death'[3]. There is no doubt she was preserved so that she could give birth to the son who was to set England on fire in the next century.

Born in London on 20th January 1669, Susanna was the youngest of Dr Annesley's twenty five children. Her mother's father had also been a strong Puritan. Before the Restoration of the Monarchy he had been instrumental in removing from their posts clergymen who did not meet the high standards of Puritanism in either their morals or their attention to duty. So Puritanism was strong on both her father's and her mother's side of the family.

The worship of God was central to the Annesley household; soon after she had her talk with her father, she met with the rest of her family and the servants for a time of prayer. All members of the family and the servants were deeply committed to their faith and all had great respect for the master of the household. Susanna looked around the room before closing her eyes and listening to her father's lengthy prayer. He had a beautiful voice and she enjoyed listening to him. He was also a good preacher and although her allegiance was now to the Church of England, she had every intention of still listening to him preach at Spitalfields where he was a licensed Presbyterian 'teacher'.

The following Sunday she accompanied the family to Little St Helen's at Spitalfields, the New House that had

---

3   Ibid.

been built for the Nonconformist congregation. She had been there before but was always impressed by its size. There were three galleries and a great number of benches facing the pulpit.

Susanna glanced around her. She felt sad that the hall was bare of decoration and the few windows were clear. She preferred the stained glass windows of the Church of England. How ever plain it might be, it had witnessed drama. One day in October three years previously in 1678 the service had been rudely interrupted by a distraught woman. Susanna remembered with a thrill of horror how the woman had burst into the Hall, denouncing Dr Annesley and his congregation as 'the false Church' and accusing them of being of the 'Spirit of Antichrist'.

Susanna had recognised the woman as Elizabeth Bathurst who had once been a member of Dr Annesley's congregation but she had left to join the Society of Friends. Susanna remembered how her father had calmly asked Elizabeth to wait until the end of the service. She had remained quiet for a while but had then grown impatient and had to be forcibly removed.

No such dramatic occurrence marred the present service and Susanna was again impressed by the power of her father's preaching and his sincerity. The service was a simple one without the ritual and set prayers of the Church of England although the words used at this Communion Service were similar.

As her father handed Susanna the bread, he said gently, 'Remember the Death of Christ.' Susanna's eyes filled with tears. She always found the Communion Service very moving.

The hall was packed. Dr Annesley was a popular preacher and even the danger inherent in attending a Nonconformist service at that time did not deter the congregation and as usual hundreds had come to hear him preach.

There were not quite so many present a few months later on 3rd August 1682 when Susanna's eldest sister, Elizabeth married the bookseller and publisher, John Dunton, who was a member of Dr Annesley's congregation. Many people thought him eccentric but Susanna liked him. He was always kind to her and she knew Elizabeth loved him. Before the church service the wedding party gathered in the hall at Spitalfields to hear the bride's father preach on the Epistle to the Ephesians chapter five and verses thirty two and thirty three. 'This is a great mystery: but I speak concerning Christ and the Church. Nevertheless let every one of you in particular so love his wife even as himself; and the wife see that she reverence her husband.'

Susanna was thirteen and she had waited eagerly for this day. She listened attentively to the sermon and then followed the bride and groom and the rest of the wedding party to Allhallows the Wall Church where they exchanged their wedding vows. As Susanna listened, she wondered how long it would be before she, too, stood at the altar.

Elizabeth looked lovely. She was tall with light chestnut coloured hair and dark eyes. Her fair complexion was set off by her gold silk bodice and skirt. The silk had been bought in Spitalfields near her home. The Huguenots, French Protestants who had fled from their native country to escape persecution, had recently introduced the silk trade to England.

Elizabeth's skirt was looped back with a bunch of coloured ribbons to show an underskirt of pale gold; the bodice was laced at the front and the round neckline trimmed with lace. Her full sleeves reached to the wrist and ended in frilled lace cuffs which cascaded over her bare hands which held a bouquet of roses, pansies and violets. On her feet were matching high heeled shoes. Her hair had been freshly curled and was decorated with bunches of coloured ribbons. On her head she wore the newly fashionable fontage head-dress. Lace and ribbons attached to a small cap were wired up high on her head while ribbons from the back dangled over her shoulders.

Ribbons had become very popular and even the bridegroom's breeches were decorated with them. Standing behind her sister, Susanna looked down complacently at her small hands encased in the lace trimmed gloves John Dunton had given her as a memento of the wedding day. Each of her sisters had also received a pair. She knew that it was the custom for gifts of gloves or ribbons to be given to wedding guests.

The service ended and Susanna and the rest of the wedding party followed the bride and groom back to the house where the reception rooms soon became thronged with people. Some of them Susanna had already met at her father's table and she had enjoyed talking to them. She did not know that her sister's wedding was also the day she was to meet her future husband for the first time.

Long tables had been set out and the smell of the food mingled with that of the summer flower arrangements. Roses, violets, daisies and pansies were intertwined with colourful ribbons to decorate the tables. There was plenty of food and the noise grew as the guests ate and chatted. Susanna ignored the popular beef and mustard and helped herself to some frumenty, wheat boiled in milk and seasoned with cinnamon and sugar.

After the customary speeches there was a lull in the proceedings and then before the chatter could start again, a short, stocky young man stepped forward.

"I wish to add my congratulations to the happy couple and in grateful thanks for all the bridegroom has done for me, I should like to read a poem I have written in honour of the marriage."

Susanna listened with interest and later as her new brother-in-law passed near her, she said, "Who is your poet, brother John?"

The bridegroom paused. "His name is Samuel Wesley. I have published some of his work."

"He is grateful then. Will you not introduce me to him?"

"Of course."

The poet was standing by himself and turned as John and Susanna came up.

John nodded to the young man. "Susanna, may I present Samuel Wesley, a very good friend of mine. Samuel, you have not met Mistress Susanna, Elizabeth's youngest sister."

Samuel bowed and Susanna curtseyed. "I am honoured to meet you, Mistress Susanna," said the young man.

"The honour is mine, Sir. Your *epithalamium*[4] was charming. I know my sister appreciated it."

He looked pleased. "Thank you, mistress."

"You have not been to my father's house before, Sir?"

"No, but I hope I shall have the honour of visiting again."

"You will be most welcome, Sir. I should enjoy talking with you."

He looked startled at this comment from a young girl but she seemed quite serious. He did not know that her father had encouraged her to take part in discussions from an early age and she had an agile mind. He decided to test her; he knew her father held strong Dissenter views.

"I have to tell you, mistress, that I am a lapsed Dissenter who is now a convinced High Churchman."

---

4   Poem composed in honour of a wedding

Susanna smiled. "I, too, have High Church leanings although my father holds other views."

"And what does your father say to that?" he asked, amused. There was more to this young lady than he had suspected.

Before she could reply, a piercing shriek followed by violent sobbing startled the guests into silence.

"Excuse me," Susanna said politely to Samuel as she identified the sound and made her way towards a small boy crouching in a corner and crying. She reached him at the same time as his mother.

"My — my ribbon," he wailed. "My ribbon. It is gone."

"Oh dear." His mother looked helplessly round as if she could conjure a new ribbon out of the air. Susanna was more practical.

"You've lost the ribbon the bridegroom gave you?"

He nodded and his sobs quietened. "Want ribbon."

"Never mind," said Susanna briskly. "See. You can have mine. Aren't they pretty?"

She unpinned the bunch of coloured ribbons from the front of her dress and handed it to him. His crying stopped immediately. He grabbed them from her hand.

"Pretty. Pretty," he cooed.

His mother looked flustered. "But they are yours."

Susanna smiled. "I was also given some gloves as a memento. I shall not miss the ribbons."

"That is very kind of you. Come, Richard. Would you like some mince pie and custard?"

She led her offspring away and Susanna moved back to the table and helped herself to some Banbury cake which had recently become popular. Inside some plain dough she tasted a richer filling mixed with currants. It was very rich. The festivities went on for a long while and she enjoyed watching the people and thinking about the young man she had just met. She hoped they would meet again.

Later that year a more unpleasant event occurred. Susanna had always known there was an element of danger for her father in being a Dissenter. The authorities were determined that the Church of England should be the only recognised church and condoned the persecution of those who did not agree with them. Nonconformists were often fined for holding meetings and sometimes their houses were raided and their goods seized to pay the fines. Dr Annesley did not escape this fate.

On Saturday November 18th 1682 Susanna was sitting reading while her elder sister, Judith, sewed. Suddenly there was a tremendous crash and a voice shouted, "Open in the name of the King."

"Oh dear. Whatever is that?" Susanna flew towards the door.

"Stop. It may be dangerous." Judith seized her arm.

"But Papa might be in danger." Susanna wrenched her arm away and opened the door on a frightening scene. Her father had come out of his study and a burly constable and three other men were manhandling him out of the way. She ran to help him but one of the men blocked her way.

"Stay out of the way, mistress, and you won't get hurt," he growled.

"But what are you doing? Pray don't hurt Papa. He has done nothing wrong."

"He doesn't recognise the Church of England and he preaches Dissension. His goods are to be seized to replace the fine he has not paid."

The constable pushed Dr Annesley out of the way and Susanna put out her hands to stop him falling. Judith was still cowering in the doorway. She gave a cry of distress as a pottery dish that had belonged to their mother crashed to the floor and one of the men stamped on it. He laughed brutally and turned to pick up some valuable silver candlesticks. Then he and his companions rampaged through the house seizing as much as they could carry.

But at last the raid was over and they gave a last kick to the broken door as they left.

"Are you all right, Papa?" Susanna looked anxiously at her father. He was breathing heavily but did not appear to be hurt.

"I am not injured my child. I am sorry you had to witness such a thing."

"They have damaged so much," mourned Judith. "There was no need for that."

"No," her father agreed. "And they took more than they need have done. I know what the legal fine is and those candlesticks alone are worth far more. But at least we are safe."

It took some considerable time to restore order to the house and it was an event Susanna never forgot.

CHAPTER TWO

An Enlightened Mother

Samuel Wesley became a frequent visitor to the Annesley's house and Susanna enjoyed her discussions with him. One midday dinner she was delighted to find herself seated next to him at the table. Young though she was, she had become very attracted to him. Like herself, he was a deep thinker and she loved hearing him discourse.

"You told me you are attracted to the Church of England, Mistress Susanna," he said politely.

Susanna was no shrinking violet and was delighted to share her views with this very personable young man.

"Yes indeed, Mr Wesley. I heard Mr Beveridge speak of the beauty of the Book of Common Prayer and I was much moved."

"He is a fine speaker. Does your father not object to your allegiance to the Church of England which he rejects?"

"Papa is very kind. He accepts my decision and understands my point of view as I understand his."

"You are fortunate indeed in such a father." Samuel turned his attention to his plate of Dutch pudding, a delicious dish made of minced beef, breadcrumbs and spices.

Susanna was disappointed. She wanted to continue to talk to him. Glancing sideways at him, as she took a mouthful of beef, she wondered if she could raise an issue that had been exercising her recently. Perhaps he could help her to make up her mind.

"Mr Wesley," she began hesitantly, "what do you think of the view of those who deny the existence of the Trinity and the divinity of Christ? I believe their doctrine is called Socinianism."

Startled, Samuel swallowed a mouthful of pudding too quickly and almost choked. Hurriedly sipping some wine, he turned a fierce look upon her.

"I think nothing of them, mistress." He looked grim.

"But why, Sir? Will you not give me your reasons? I have read their writings and they seem to me to be logical. How can one God be three persons?"

"It is a mystery that we must accept," he said more gently. "We know there is a great Creator God. The evidence is all around us in the beauty of nature. We know that he sent his Son into the world as a Man and …"

Susanna interrupted. "But how can the omnipotent God become a mere man? It is so difficult to comprehend."

"Yes, I agree it is difficult. One has to have faith. Remember the Scriptures tell us 'there is one mediator between God and man — the man Christ Jesus.' "

"But how do we *know* he was the Son of God?"

"The evidence is irrefutable. Do you not believe in the Resurrection?"

"Yes. I have to."

"Then who but God could break the power of death?

'Behold the Saviour of Mankind
Nailed to the shameful tree.
How vast the love that Him inclined
To bleed and die for me.' "

Susanna was silent. Her lips curved in a smile as the fire of her companion's fervour started to dissolve her doubts. But she had one more question.

"And the third person of the Trinity?"

"Would we be able to speak of the Lord and what he has done were it not for the Holy Spirit? Remember how the disciples changed at Pentecost when the tongues of fire came upon them. Oh Susanna, you must believe this."

Startled at the unexpected use of her name, she turned to look at him. Their eyes met and locked before he looked away. She gave a sigh of happiness as she whispered, "You have convinced me, Sir."

"I am glad," he answered gruffly. He spoke no more but helped himself to some cheese.

Susanna had much to think about. She was glad she had spoken to him about her doubts. She had never met anyone like him before. Over the next few years their friendship blossomed and developed into love but Samuel was not yet in a position to maintain a wife so they were not able to get married.

In 1688, when Susanna was eighteen, a momentous event occurred about which she felt very strongly. James II of the House of Stuart was deposed. The throne was offered to Prince William of Orange who was married to James' elder daughter, Mary. William accepted the Crown and became William III. Susanna was disturbed by this. She considered no one had the right to force from his throne a king who ruled by the 'Divine Right of Kings'[5]. In her opinion, William was a usurper and had no right to wrest the throne from the rightful king.

She was disappointed to discover Samuel did not share her views about this; many clergy who agreed with her, refused to take the Oath of allegiance to the new King. Unable to discuss the subject with Samuel, Susanna's journal became the recipient of her views. Sitting down at her desk one afternoon she wrote:

'Whether they did well in driving a prince from his hereditary throne, I leave to their own consciences to determine; though I cannot tell how to think that a king of England can ever be accountable to his subjects for any maladministrations or abuse of power: but as he derives his power from God, so to Him only must he answer of his using it. But whether the praying for a usurper, and vindicating his usurpation after he has the throne, be not participating (in) his sins, is easily determined.' [6]

This particular point later caused a serious rift between Samuel and Susanna but their disagreement did not reach its peak until some time later. At this time they continued to discuss theological topics and found they were in agreement on most of them.

In 1689 Samuel was ordained and for a few months he served as a naval chaplain with the handsome stipend of seventy pounds a year. But he preferred to be a civilian and he missed Susanna so he resigned his commission and obtained a curacy in St Botolph's Church, Aldersgate at the much lower salary of thirty pounds a year. However, he was still writing and was able to double his stipend with his published work.

---

5   This was the view held at the time. The King ruled by 'Divine Right' so no one had the right to depose him.

6   The Wesley Banner (1852)

He felt he was now in a position to marry the beautiful girl he had first met at her sister's wedding. They were married towards the end of 1689 when Susanna was nineteen.

From her luxurious home Susanna moved with her new husband into some 'mean lodgings' in Holborn. Once married, Samuel did not find the time to talk with his new bride as he had once done. He was too busy writing and living in his dream world. It was Susanna who had her feet firmly planted on the ground but she was disappointed she rarely saw her husband. She had been a rebel in her father's house and had disputed his teaching but her tolerant father had accepted her views and been proud that she thought for herself. Not so Samuel. Although at first they had been in agreement about most things, afterwards it was obvious to Susanna that Samuel expected her always to accept his views so that he could hold 'undisputed sway' in his house. Susanna was expected to obey him in all things.

This was, of course, the seventeenth century view of marriage but Susanna had been brought up by a liberal father who was in advance of this time and she objected to Samuel's 'chains' and the lack of time he spent with her.

"Can you not spend more time with me, Samuel?" she pleaded one cold December day.

"I would like to, my dear, but I have to write to earn enough money for us to live on."

"We never have time now to talk about things as we once did," said his wife sadly.

"We will again. Never fear."

But the curate spent most of his time alone in his study writing to supplement his low stipend. In 1690 his brother-in-law, John Dunton, produced a magazine called the *Athenian Gazette*, published three times a week. Samuel contributed to it on a regular basis and this helped to boost his meagre salary.

A few months later, Susanna had news for her husband. "I am expecting our child, Samuel," she told him one evening before he could rush off to hide himself in his study.

His eyes lit up. "Our son shall be a clergyman and follow in the footsteps of his father and grandfathers. He will be a credit to the Wesleys and the Annesleys."

There was no doubt in his mind that the child would be a boy.

Susanna smiled. "What shall we call him, husband?"

"Who but 'Samuel'? It is my name and the son should be named after his father."

Susanna bowed her head. "My father's name was also Samuel. It is a good name. Pray God he lives up to it."

A few days later as Susanna was doing some embroidery and Samuel was, for once, sitting with her, she suddenly sighed and put down her work.

"O, Samuel," she exclaimed. "I have a great craving for mulberries. Would that we could grow some."

"Some time we shall have some," he promised.

The next day he came back with some for her but refused to say where he had obtained them.

"That is so kind of you, Samuel," she said gratefully as she popped two in her mouth and the juice ran down her chin. She knew that often husbands whose wives were pregnant took over much of the management of the house until after the child was born. However she knew she could not expect Samuel to help. Even if he were willing, he would probably forget what he was supposed to be doing while he struggled for the right word in his latest poem.

As the time approached, Susanna knew that her baby could not be born in the tiny lodging house where they were living.

"Samuel, I wish to return to my father's house for the birth," she told her husband.

He looked worried. "You feel — well, Sukey?"

She smiled. "I am fine but there will be women there to help me."

"Yes. You are right. You will have a licensed midwife?" He sounded anxious.

"I think it matters not whether she is licensed. Many good midwives are not. There is one, Mrs Ellis, who has delivered many children. She will assist me. I know not if she is licensed."

She hoped Samuel would not make a fuss. Midwives were supposed to obtain licenses to practise. This involved taking an oath administered by the Bishop. However, in practice a great many midwives practised without being licensed. As Susanna did not know Mrs Ellis' status, Samuel gave her the benefit of the doubt and as her time drew near, Susanna returned to her father's house to await the birth of her firstborn.

She had prepared carefully and took with her clean clothes and fresh bedding. As was the custom, she had a large white linen sheet which would cover the bed on which she would give birth. A maid, Agnes, helped her prepare the room for the birth. The bed was moved into the middle of the room so that the women who assisted her might be able to move around easily. Mrs Ellis would bring assistants with her.

"It must not be near the door, mistress," Agnes announced. "There must be no draughts to harm you or the child."

"And close to the fire for warmth," added Susanna.

They shifted the bed and Agnes helped Susanna lay the white sheet over it. Soon after this, Susanna's pains started and Mrs Ellis was sent for. There was no privacy for Susanna at the birth of her first child. As well as Mrs Ellis and her assistants, two of Susanna's sisters were also in attendance. Susanna was soon unaware of anything except excruciating pain. The room, even in February, was stifling and she could hardly breathe. Custom demanded that the doors and windows of the birth room should be shut to avoid draughts as cold air was thought to be harmful. It was also dim and gloomy to simulate the dark snugness of the womb so the child should not be shocked by bright light when he or she emerged into the world.

"There, there, dear," soothed Mrs Ellis, bathing her patient's face as Susanna screamed. "Drink this. It will ease the pain and speed the birth."

What herbal remedies were in the brew Susanna neither knew nor cared. It was probably tansy and sage, a common remedy for pregnant women. She sipped a little before the pain came again. Mrs Ellis was beginning to look flustered but her hands, carefully rubbed with oil of lilies, were gentle as she tried to help the distraught woman to give birth.

After many hours her ministrations were successful and the wailing of a child pierced the gloom. Beaming, the midwife removed the child from Susanna, competently cut the cord and proceeded to clean the little body before swaddling it in bands of clean cloth. The women cooed as they peered at the tiny face peeping out from the white linen.

"You have a beautiful son, Mrs Wesley," Mrs Ellis told her patient laying the tiny boy in the mother's arms.

Susanna smiled. "Thank God. Please call my husband."

Samuel, who had been pacing the floor below while his wife laboured above, was called and taking the child from Susanna, Mrs Ellis handed him to Samuel, saying, "Reverend Wesley, here is your son. May God give you much joy of him."

Hesitantly, Samuel took the tiny figure and looked proudly down at his firstborn. He smiled at his wife who was obviously exhausted. "How are you, Sukey?"

"I am well, husband. He is beautiful, is he not?"

"He certainly is." Samuel returned the child to the midwife who put him in the crib. Samuel looked shyly at his wife. "I am so glad our firstborn was a boy ."

"You will have many more fine sons," beamed Mrs Ellis. Susanna frowned but made no comment. It had been a difficult birth and she was not sure she wanted to go through the experience again.

She stayed for another six weeks in her father's house enjoying being the focus of attention and receiving visits from her sisters and neighbours. Soon after she returned to Holborn, Sammy, as their son came to be called, was baptised in his father's church while Susanna tried to adjust to her new life. But she missed the bustle and chat of her father's house and became very depressed. Now that Sammy was safely born, Samuel reverted to his old ways and spent little time with his wife. Susanna turned increasingly to her God for help and continued to write her thoughts in her journal.

Four months after Sammy was born, his father had some news.

"The Marquis of Normanby has offered me a Living in South Ormsby, Sukey!" he exclaimed. "I think I should accept it."

Susanna looked bewildered. "Where is South Ormsby, husband?"

"It is in Lincolnshire."

"That is far from London. I shall be sorry to leave the city. I have lived here all my life."

"The country air will be better for the child."

She could not fault that argument and she knew she had to go where her husband wished. It was a long journey in the carriage through the centre of England. Susanna had never left the bustling city of London and the deserted countryside was strange to her. Little Samuel was crying and she hugged him tightly. She felt like crying herself as she left her roots behind not knowing if she would ever return. It was to be over thirty years before she saw the capital city again. But she stiffened her back and tried to smile at her husband. His stipend would be the same but she hoped it might be cheaper to live in Lincolnshire.

"Here we are. See what a pretty village it is." Samuel's voice broke into her thoughts.

Susanna looked through the window. It was indeed picturesque with its little cottages and green fields clustering around the ancient church that was to be Samuel's domain. She handed the baby to his father and clambered down from the carriage. Her heart sank as they went into the Parsonage. It was little better than a mud hut, she thought. It was damp and through the clay walls could be seen the reed frame. Work would need to be done on it to make it habitable.

Having cast a cursory look around his new abode, Samuel announced he had to go to the Hall to pay his respects to his patron, Lord Castleton, the Marquis of Normanby.

"It is, after all, through his good offices I have the living," he reminded his wife.

Susanna nodded. She was already deciding what had to be done to make the Parsonage comfortable. When her husband returned, he was not in the best of tempers. Susanna was by now used to his fiery temper but this time she knew it was not caused by anything she had said or done. He flung himself into a chair and glared at her.

"Lord Castleton has made me his private chaplain. I think he expects me to be at his call whenever he needs me."

"You didn't like him very much?" ventured Susanna.

"I don't like his style of living, Sukey. He is the patron of the Living and the leading churchman in the district and yet he does not live as a Christian." He paused and then shot his wife an angry look. "He has a lady living there to whom he is not married. I do not approve."

"No dear," agreed his wife. "That is indeed very wrong." On that issue they were certainly at one.

Life at South Ormsby was not easy. The population was about two hundred but Samuel was not typical of rural clergy of that time. Most of them were happy to spend their days playing bowls or shovelboard, doing odd jobs and working on their glebes[7]. Although Samuel had to work his glebe with the assistance of his wife, he spent more time in his study working and writing. Most clergymen were content to be at the beck and call of their patrons whose style of life was often not consistent with Christianity. It was rarely they were called to account by their Chaplains but Samuel found it very hard to condone immorality.

"I am forced to see drinking and gaming and dare not open my mouth against it," he told Susanna in disgust. "I am taken little notice of in matters of religion and I fear that if I do speak, it would occasion nothing but my removal from the family. In the meantime, unless I do remonstrate, I think I do not do what becomes a minister of religion. I may even be justly condemned as a partaker in another man's sin."

---

7   Portion of land that went with a clergyman's benefice.

"I am sure that would not be the case, Samuel," said Susanna soothingly. "But the pulpit is a privileged place from where custom has given you authority to speak. Surely, therefore, you may discharge your duty without fear."

Samuel sighed. "You are right. I will try to do my duty." He returned to work in his study leaving his wife to continue her work.

Never afraid of hard work, she had thrown herself whole-heartedly into her new role. On her, fell the burden of running the household as Samuel still spent most of his days writing in his study. Susanna was soon homesick; she missed the bustle of London and she still yearned for the stimulating discussions she had once listened to in her father's house. Even Samuel never discussed theology with her now.

However she had little time to indulge in nostalgic dreams. In spite of her hard time with the first birth she became pregnant again and a little daughter was born soon after they arrived in South Ormsby; sadly, the baby lived only a few months. The following year Emilia was born and to Susanna's relief she survived and was baptised on 13th January 1692. Two years later little twin brothers were born. Named Annesley and Jedidiah, they were baptised on 3rd December but died the following year.

Fortunately, another daughter was born in 1695. Named after her mother—and nicknamed 'Sukey'—she survived. Soon after thee birth, Susanna spoke to her husband of her concern about Samuel junior, their eldest son.

"He does not speak yet, Samuel," she told her husband. "He is more than four years old. He should speak."

"He is fit in every other way," said Samuel, frowning. "He understands and obeys. Pray God he is not to be dumb all his life."

"Oh don't say so, husband," Susanna cried. "I could not bear it. I could not face my firstborn having to suffer so."

"We can but pray. If it is the Lord's will, so be it."

Samuel left his wife to her thoughts. They were not happy. There was a special bond between the mother and this little son of her 'extremest sorrow'. He had given her such pain in his birth and now in his childhood he was still causing her anxiety. She gazed at him sadly. He must be taught but how could she teach him if he would not speak.

He was a solitary child and had befriended a little cat that had appeared one day in the house. He carried it about with him and often hid with it from his family. They were used to his disappearances and did not worry unduly. But on 10th February 1695, his fifth birthday, he was missing for several hours. Susanna was frantic. She searched the house and went out into the fields calling and calling.

"Even if he hears, he cannot answer," she thought sadly.

She sat down in the rocking chair in the kitchen and buried her face in her hands. "Oh God, protect my son. Guard him where he is and bring him safely back to me," she prayed.

After her prayer, she felt a little calmer. Her hands were idle in her lap and three year old Emilia was crawling round her skirts.

"Oh Sammy, where are you?" she sighed.

"Here I am, mother."

Susanna jumped. Her heart started to pound and she thought she must be dreaming. She had heard a voice but could see no one.

"Sammy," she whispered.

The tablecloth covering the kitchen table quivered and a little face appeared underneath it. The face was followed by a small body as her eldest son crawled out from under the table clutching his beloved cat. He stood up and came towards his mother, carefully placing his pet on the floor.

"Oh Sammy." Susanna hugged him—an unusual occurrence. She was not given to demonstrations of affection. "You naughty boy. Why did you hide from Mama? Did you not hear me calling?"

He nodded, grinning at her. "Yes, Mama."

She hugged him again. Her anxiety of the past few hours was forgotten. Samuel could talk! His words were perfectly articulated and at last Susanna decided she would be able to teach him to read.

The next day she started his education — a pattern she was to follow with the rest of her children. Emilia was left in the kitchen and Joan, the nurse, was told to watch her.

"No one is to disturb us," Susanna instructed the nurse. "I am to teach my son his letters. Come, Sammy."

Her husband was out so Susanna led her son into the Rector's study and sat him down in front of the desk while she sat beside him.

"Now, Samuel, you are to learn the alphabet. Say after me: A — B — C — D ..."

He was an apt pupil. Bright and intelligent, he was eager to learn. He repeated the alphabet after her. By midday, he could say it from memory and he knew the different sounds and how they were used in words. Susanna was delighted.

"He will do well," she told his pleased father that evening. "He will fulfil all our hopes and follow in his father's footsteps. He learnt the alphabet in just a few hours. He learns quickly."

The following day, the young boy was shown the first chapter of the book of Genesis. Susanna pointed to the first verse. "Read the letters, Sammy," she instructed. He did so correctly. "Now look at the words. Look at them as I read and then repeat them: *In the beginning God created the heaven and the earth.*"

"In the ... be-be-gin- ning God ... cre-created the heaven and the ... earth."

"Good. Now say it again and again, until you can read it without any hesitation."

The second time was better and soon there were no pauses.

"Now the second verse." His mother read it and he repeated it in the same way. By the end of the lesson, he could read ten verses fluently and within a few weeks he could read a whole chapter. He continued to read the Bible and was also introduced to other books that Susanna considered suitable.

"He has such a prodigious memory," Susanna told her husband. "I cannot remember ever to have told him the same word twice. He reads continually and any word he has learnt in his lesson, he knows again whenever he sees it, either in his Bible or any other book. He can now read an English author very well."

Susanna was expecting another baby so Sammy was left to continue his education alone for a short while. This was no hardship to him as he loved reading and was extending his knowledge of the Bible every day. Susanna's new daughter was named after her mother and the following year in 1696 yet another daughter was born to Samuel and Susanna. She was named Mary. Susanna was by now exhausted with childbearing and a nurse was employed to look after the children. But she was careless.

One day she came to Susanna in great distress. "Oh Ma'am, I have done a wicked thing. I dropped the baby and I think she is hurt."

Susanna's heart almost stopped as she took the tiny baby from the nurse. The baby was not crying but her eyes were wide open and one side of her little body had become twisted. Susanna's eyes filled with tears as she hugged her daughter. There was no money to spare for a physician and there was little he would be able to do. Little Mary was to grow up with a deformed body but a beautiful face and loveable character. This was one more cross Susanna had to bear.

Life was hard as Susanna tried to run the household with little help from her husband. She still managed to keep to her daily routine of meditation and prayer from six to seven in the evening; she regarded this as one of the most important aspects of her life. A born manager, she organised her large household as well as she could. But even she was not able to conjure money out of air and they were soon in debt. Samuel's writing brought in a little extra but it was not enough to feed and clothe a growing family.

"What are we to do, Samuel?" sighed Susanna. "We become more in debt every day."

Samuel looked shamefaced. "'Tis partly my own fault, I think," he said. "I am no expert in money matters. I know I do not manage well. We will have to borrow."

Neither of them liked to do this but there was no alternative. Samuel soon forgot about the problem and immersed himself in his books. But the Marquis's loose morals soon became too much for Samuel to accept. Lord Castleton's mistress had taken to visiting Susanna. When Samuel discovered this, he was horrified.

"My dear, I wish you not to be so intimate with her. She is not fit company for you."

Susanna's eyes flashed and her mouth tightened. It was not easy to turn someone away from her door.

"Fit company she may not be but how can I refuse to let her in? She is lonely when the Marquis is away. She likes to talk. I assure you her conversation is of the most sedate."

Samuel glared at his wife, his temper rising. "I do not wish to entertain her in my house. The morals at the Hall are not of the sort to encroach upon a Parson's family."

Susanna gave a mocking laugh. "May I remind you, my dear, that it is the Marquis of Normanby who is your patron. It was through his good offices you received this living. Surely you do not wish to offend him by refusing to allow his lady to visit."

"If she was his 'lady', it would be a different matter. But she is not married to him as you well know. I do not wish her to enter my home." Samuel's voice rose. "You are my wife and you will obey me." He flung himself out of the house slamming the door. The draught caused smoke from the fire to seep into the room.

Susanna gave a sigh which turned into a cough. She wished Samuel were not so difficult. The life led by the Marquis of Normanby and his lady was not one of which she approved either but her natural kindliness prevented her from turning the lady away. But one day, she was sure there would be an explosion. It came sooner than she expected.

The following day she was sitting in the kitchen while the children were having their afternoon sleep. For once it was quiet. Picking up Mary's petticoat from the pile of mending that lay on the table beside her, she started to repair the tear that the tiny deformed baby had made in her efforts to walk. A knock at the door startled her. Opening it, she found on the doorstep the lady of ill repute whose visits Samuel had forbidden. Susanna hesitated only briefly.

"Come in," she said quietly. "Do sit down."

Lord Castleton's mistress sat herself down on the chair Susanna had just vacated and stretched out her beringed fingers to the fire.

"Brr. It is cold out there and I am weary from the walk. How are you, Mistress Wesley?"

"I am well, I thank you." Susanna sat down in one of the upright wooden chairs.

"And the children? Your husband?"

"Well too."

"You are blest in them." Fashionable and wealthy though she was, there was sadness in the visitor's voice.

Susanna hastened to change the subject. "Can I offer you some soup?" There was little enough for the family in the pot on the stove but as a good hostess, she had to offer it. Briefly she remembered the life that she had lived in her father's house. That now seemed luxury.

To her relief her visitor shook her head. "Thank you, no. We have but just dined. I am replete." She patted her stomach.

Susanna's lips twitched. There was no doubt the lady was rather vulgar but she was good hearted and the Parson's wife was sure her refusal owed as much to the knowledge of her hostess's poverty as to her recent meal.

"Lord Castleton is well?"

"Thank you. He is in good health. We have visitors at the Hall." She learnt forward confidentially. "I have escaped to have a cosy chat with you, Mistress. There are such things planned."

The narrative that followed was no doubt expurgated but Susanna hoped that her children would remain asleep until her visitor left. That was to be sooner than she expected. The lady was in full flow when the door flew open and the Rector stood there, glaring.

"Madam," he boomed. "You are not welcome in my house."

Before Susanna could remonstrate, he swept across to the chair, grabbed the lady's hand, almost dragged her to the door and pushed her out, slamming the door after her.

"Samuel, how could you be so ill mannered?" Susanna remonstrated angrily.

"I have told you, wife. She is no fit companion for you. I am going to work and do not wish to be disturbed."

"Lord Castleton will not be pleased," Susanna shouted after him. "You have done yourself no favours."

She was right. The following day the Marquis sent for Samuel. What passed between them Susanna never knew but the Wesley family was no longer welcome in the parish. A new Living had to be found.

Samuel still spent much of his life in a world of his own, writing poetry and dissertations while his wife had to cope with the practicalities of looking after the family, running the house and making the fifty pounds they received annually feed and clothe them all. The Rector had at last completed his heroic poem on 'The Life of our blessed Lord and Saviour Jesus Christ' and it was published in 1693. He dedicated it to Queen Mary who died the following year.

Samuel was convinced it was through the good offices of the Queen just before she died in 1694 that he was now offered the living of St Andrew's in Epworth in the north of Lincolnshire.

"I am minded to take it, Sukey," he told his wife. "It is worth two hundred pounds."

"That seems a lot, husband, but we shall still have difficulty, I think."

"It is right to go," he insisted.

"Yes, it has to be." Susanna, who had been sitting, sewing, stood up.

"Sukey."

She turned. "Yes, husband?"

He hesitated. "I think — I am minded to take my mother with us. She is old and frail — and I think she must go to prison if I do not assist her."

"Oh, Samuel." Susanna sighed.

"My father left her ill provided for. She has helped both me and my brother Matthew as well as she was able. I would not like her to go to prison for debt."

"No, of course not!" exclaimed his horrified wife. "She must come with us. I know too well how little a clergyman receives for his work."

Hurriedly she left the room wishing she could recall her last remark. It had not been kind to remind her husband that she, too, was suffering from poverty. She sighed again, knowing that to her would fall the task of packing up and organising the move to the place she would live for the next thirty eight years. She was also pregnant again.

But before they moved they received some sad news. Dr Annesley, Susanna's father had died. Susanna was devastated. She had been very close to her father although she did not agree with all his views. When she left London, she had known she would probably not see him again in this world but that did not lessen her grief. However, with her usual serenity, she put her feelings to one side and concentrated on preparing for her new life.

CHAPTER THREE

An Unpopular Rector

Susanna was exhausted before they started the long journey to Epworth. It was only a short way as the crow flies but she knew it would take them some time because for most of the journey the coach would have to travel across fields as there were not roads worthy of the name in that part of the county. The baby inside her was starting to make itself felt and she felt uncomfortable but, stoical as ever, she would never admit to pain. She hoped the jolting of the coach would not cause the baby to come prematurely.

She sighed as she bundled the children into the coach before her. It was a bitterly cold day and they had been fractious all morning. Poor little deformed Mary was still crying quietly but Susanna ignored her. Emilia was sulky at leaving the only home she had ever known, little five year old Sukey was shivering with cold and only Sammy at seven was trying to behave like a man.

The coach door slammed and they were off. Susanna glanced back at the house she had lived in for the past seven years. Life at South Ormsby had been hard. She hoped Epworth would be an improvement but she was a realist so she knew things would not change very much. She looked at her mother-in-law whose head was already nodding.

Before long the coach left the road and jolted on to the fields. The occupants of the coach were flung from side to side and Susanna winced as she bounced on the wooden seat. She felt the baby inside her express its disapproval. Turning her face away from her family to hide her pain, she stared disconsolately at the barren landscape.

A thought came to her and she shuddered. Shutting her eyes, she prayed earnestly that no highwaymen would accost them. She knew there were many in the area who held up unsuspecting travellers. However, she thought grimly, there would be small pickings from the occupants of this particular coach. They hardly had enough to live on and Samuel was always in debt. It was not his fault. A country rector did not earn enough to keep his family in any style. Fleetingly Susanna remembered the luxury of her father's house which she had left to marry Samuel. She rarely thought now of her previous life style. She did not believe in self pity.

A particularly vicious jolt caused her to clutch her stomach and she bit her lips to stop herself crying out. She grabbed Mary before she rolled off the seat and made sure the rest of them were safe. Glancing at Emilia, she saw that her eldest daughter was trying not to cry but she had no intention of showing any sympathy. The child must learn that life was hard and one had to suffer whatever God had in store for them.

For a while the jolting was regular but the false sense of security was shattered as the coach suddenly lurched and then shuddered to a halt.

"Oh dear!" exclaimed Susanna. "What has happened?"

"Don't worry, my dear," said her husband calmly. "The wheels will have stuck in a rut. We'll get help." He clambered out of the coach with difficulty as it had tilted dangerously to one side. "Come children. We have to wait outside."

He held out his arms as Susanna strained to push each child towards him. Lastly he helped out his wife and his mother. It had been cold in the coach but once outside, the chill wind pierced right through their threadbare clothes. Susanna clutched her shabby cloak around her with one hand and tried to prevent the mischievous wind from snatching her bonnet from her head. Some of her hair had escaped from its pins and was trailing down her cheeks but even her dowdy clothes and the strain around her eyes and mouth could not detract from the beauty for which she had been justly famous.

Miserably, she and the children waited with their grandmother, trying to huddle behind the coach to shelter from the bitter wind. It seemed an age before Samuel returned with a ruddy-cheeked farmer leading two strong looking cart horses. The animals gave the impression that pulling coaches out of ditches was all in their day's work. It probably was! Their own horses stood quietly while the vast beasts were roped to the coach and gradually with a sucking sound, the wheels were freed and the coach was righted.

"Thank you, my friend," said Samuel warmly. "We are in your debt."

The farmer touched his cap which had stayed on his head in spite of the wind. "I'm glad to 'elp you, Sir — and your lady."

Susanna nodded graciously to him and the family struggled back into the coach.

"How much further is it, father?" asked Sammy.

"We have some way to go yet. Don't worry, my son. We shall arrive safely. God will take care of us."

"Yes, father." His son stared glumly out of the window. He was tired, cold and hungry but he knew better than to complain.

As they travelled on, the road disappeared altogether. The carriage bumped across fields of barley and rye, crushing the crops under the wheels. Susanna wondered whose crops they were destroying. There were two more unpleasant upsets before they finally reached their destination.

Epworth was situated in the centre of the recently drained swamp of the Isle of Axholme. The low lying district was bounded by three rivers, the Trent, the Don and the Idle. The small market town, which was to become famous throughout the world because of its connection with the Wesleys was set on the side of a small hill. When the new Rector arrived there, it boasted about two thousand inhabitants.

As the carriage bumped to a halt, Susanna straightened her bonnet, pushed her hair under it and stepped out to walk up the path to their new home. Lifting her head high, she gazed with thoughtful interest at the parsonage that was to become one of the most famous in the world.

"It looks better than our previous abode, husband," she observed.

"Indeed it does," he agreed enthusiastically. "We are starting a new life, Sukey."

She smiled affectionately at him. Dear Samuel. Always so enthusiastic but with little idea of the difficulties his wife had to overcome in order to make him comfortable. But that was a woman's role — to care for her husband and children. Her lips twitched as she remembered their frequent arguments. Both strong-willed, neither would give way and the air around them was often full of the sparks of their anger. But in spite of all, they loved each other deeply.

Looking at her new home, her spirits lifted. It was indeed a palace compared with the parsonage at South Ormsby. Built attractively of timber and plaster, the roof was thatched and the many windows suggested a number of rooms. She noticed that some of the windows were boarded up. The previous year a tax on windows had been introduced and many people had boarded up some of their windows to reduce this. She was glad this had been done on their new home and wondered if they could dispense with any other windows. There were so many the tax would be very high and they had little enough to live on. The Rectory was much larger than the one they had left.

"There will be more room for the children," Susanna observed as they opened the door and stepped over the threshold.

Tired though she was, she was determined to inspect her new domain. The children, also forgetting their fatigue, followed her, little Mary clutching at the hem of her skirt and shuffling along on all fours. From room to room the family marched, their enthusiasm growing.

Downstairs there was a hall, a kitchen, a parlour and a buttery where provisions would be stored.

"Can we go upstairs, Mama?" Emilia plucked at her sleeve.

Susanna smiled at her daughter. "Indeed we can but take care you don't fall down."

Picking up Mary, who was having difficulty negotiating the stairs, Susanna led the way.

"This one is so large," gasped Sammy opening one of the doors.

"And this too." Emilia peered in another.

There were several rooms on this floor and smaller ones on the floor above.

"Sukey. Come and see the garden," her husband called from downstairs.

They had forgotten the cold by now and gazed in delight at the small garden beside the stone wall.

"There's a barn too. Look!" Samuel pointed at the thatched timber and clay building.

"How much land belongs to the Rectory?" inquired Susanna.

Samuel waved his arms in the direction of the fields where grazing cows could be seen. "The glebe is about three acres. I shall be a farmer too."

Susanna wondered how her husband would cope with his new residence. The stipend for the new living was two hundred pounds—considerably more than the thirty pounds they had received at South Ormsby. But they were still in debt. Perhaps the farm would help, she reflected. She didn't mind hard work and she could learn to milk. What a challenge it would be.

Looking out over the land, she thought how desolate it looked and her depression returned. The flat marshy land stretched as far as she could see, broken only by rutted ditches and trees swaying in the wind. Susanna suspected the wind would always howl across these dreary fenlands. Across the field she could see St Andrew's Church where Samuel would spend much of his time; scattered around haphazardly were cottages and farm buildings. She wondered how large a congregation he would have and what sort of reception the new Rector and his family would receive. Perhaps it was as well on that first day she could not see into the future.

A twinge in her back reminded her that she had been on her feet for some time.

"I must sit down, Samuel," she said. Turning back to the house, she collapsed on to an old rocking chair that stood before the kitchen range.

That night the wind howled round the Rectory and the windows rattled. The next morning Susanna was up early, as usual. The Rectory was not a home yet but she would soon make it one. She went outside to find some wood to start a fire in the kitchen range. It had been raining during the night and the countryside looked as unfriendly as it had when they arrived. The wood was damp and it was some time before there was the flicker of a flame.

Filling the kettle that hung over the stove with water from the well, she added some oatmeal and hoped it would boil. Water gruel was all she had to offer her family at the moment. Later she hoped she would be able to find some barley and meat for them. She hoped the few cows grazing on the fields below might provide some milk but she didn't know how to milk them. Stirring the gruel, she wondered what the future held in store for them all. She knew Samuel's mother would stay with them for the rest of her life but she was no burden and would keep to her room for most of the time.

During the first few days Susanna and the children saw no one. No one came to welcome the new Rector and his family and they felt very isolated. Samuel rode around his parish and talked to the people but he soon realised they were not going to be popular.

"They are poor people—very different from us, Sukey," he told her one evening soon after they arrived. They had eaten their meagre supper and the children were in bed. For once they had a brief time to talk before Samuel returned to his books.

His wife gave him a direct look. "We are poor, too," she said tartly.

"But we have great riches—in books and education. I cannot get as many books as I would like but I still have some and …"

Susanna interrupted him. "Sometimes I would rather have food to put in our stomachs and no debts."

Colour flooded Samuel's face and she wondered if she had gone too far. But for once he understood. "I am truly sorry, Sukey, that you are put to such straits."

Swiftly repenting of her harsh words, she put her hand over his. "We manage. I know it is hard."

"They are a rough people with no learning. Most cannot read or write. Pray God I will be able to help them."

Samuel's way of helping was to preach fiery sermons from the pulpit urging his parishioners to repent of their wicked ways and reform their lives. The villagers, not surprisingly, became incensed and were not slow to let him know of their anger. They were already unhappy with their lot as they felt the landowners had deprived them of their rights and the new Rector's criticism added fuel to the already burning flame. Samuel's High Church services were not popular as his parishioners sympathised with the Dissenters and preferred a simpler form of worship.

Soon after the Wesleys arrived in Epworth they received news that Elizabeth Dunton, Susanna's sister, had died. Susanna was sad as she remembered the beautiful girl at whose wedding she had met her husband. But she had little time to grieve. Her baby was born soon afterwards in 1697. Their new daughter was named Methetabel — soon shortened to Hetty. She was baptised and when she had recovered from the birth, Susanna went to the church for the first of her many trips to St Andrews Church for the 'Churching of Women'. This was a service of thanksgiving that the woman had survived the perils and dangers of childbirth. The service took place whether or not the child survived. Infant mortality in the early eighteenth century was very high.

"Many of the village women refuse to be churched," Samuel complained to Susanna.

"But at least they bring their children for baptism," Susanna consoled him.

Her husband gave her a wry look. "They do not do that when they should. Sometimes they bring such monsters of men children, it almost breaks my arm to hold them."

Susanna touched his arm. "I am sorry, husband," she said gently. "Did I not know the Almighty fixes our habitation, I should think it a thousand pities that a man of your rare endowments should be confined to this obscure corner of the country where your talents are buried." [8]

Samuel was not fitted for the life of a farmer. Soon after their arrival part of the barn collapsed and had to be rebuilt, involving them in more expense. Samuel had no knowledge of farming and no capital. He appealed to some of his influential friends who gave him some money to help but the villagers realised he was no farmer and took advantage of him. The Rector's temper was short and relations with the village rapidly deteriorated. One day he returned from the market looking very flushed.

Samuel was not fitted for the life of a farmer. Soon after their arrival part of the barn collapsed and had to be rebuilt, involving them in more expense. Samuel had no knowledge of farming and no capital. He appealed to some of his influential friends who gave him some money to help but the villagers realised he was no farmer and took advantage of him. The Rector's temper was short and relations with the village rapidly deteriorated. One day he returned from the market looking very flushed.

"I found that rascally Farmer Knight cutting off the ears of my corn sheaves that I had set aside for my tithes. He was putting them into a bag and I knew he intended to sell them."

"What did you do?" asked his wife apprehensively.

---

8   Taken from some writing of Susanna's included in *The Life and Times of Samuel Wesley* by Luke Tyerman.

"I took him by the arm and marched him to the market place. Then I seized his bag and emptied it in front of the crowd. 'There, friends,' I said. 'See how Farmer Knight planned to rob me.' Then I left him to the justice of his neighbours." [9]

"Oh Samuel," sighed Susanna. "You make so many enemies."

Sometimes she thought it was like having another child to soothe. She now had five children all under seven. She was kept very busy running her household and training her children. Her husband's relations with his neighbours was yet another burden for her to bear.

Because her eldest son, Sammy, had not spoken until he was five, Susanna decided this was the age at which she would start to teach all her children. Later Sammy would have to be sent away to school but she did not want to think about that yet. However Samuel had other ideas.

"I think, my dear, our son should have a tutor," he told her one day.

"A tutor — but — "

Samuel interrupted. "There is a Mr John Holland who runs a private school in Epworth. He is prepared to take Sammy."

"But can we afford it, Samuel? We are already in debt."

Samuel ignored this. "It is very important that our son has the best education we can give him, Sukey. Mr Holland will see to that."

Susanna bowed her head. "Very well, husband."

So Samuel was enrolled at the school but he did not like it. He preferred to be taught by his mother. Susanna was not

9   ibid.

happy about it either and she had heard rumours about Mr Holland but for the moment she kept them to herself.

The day before Emilia's fifth birthday there was great activity in the Wesley household. Susanna and her little maid scrubbed and cleaned so that the house glowed with care. The children's clothes were carefully laundered so that all would be clean as the birthday morning dawned.

Susanna, as usual, was up early and did her chores before the others stirred. Then the rest of the family joined her for breakfast. Susanna (now also known as Sukey) and Mary (Molly) sat by themselves at a little table nearby so that their mother could keep an eye on them. They ate 'spoonmeat' and 'small beer'. Emilia usually sat with them but today was different.

"Emilia, today you may join us at the table. You are a big girl now."

"Oh, thank you, Mama," whispered her daughter awe-struck at the privilege.

Samuel gave thanks to God for their food and the meal was eaten quietly. The silence was broken by Sammy whispering to the maid. Susanna looked sternly at him as Betty Massey, the maid, came to her end of the table.

"Master Sammy would like some more bread, ma'am."

"Very well. You may take him some."

Usually the children were allowed to eat as much as they liked provided they did not call out for anything. They had to ask the maid who would then relay the request to their mother. Susanna kept her household on a tight rein. As it was a special day, there was cold meat on the table and also broth. Susanna had tried to make Emilia's fifth birthday a special occasion.

"May I have some beer?" Emilia whispered to Betty. The maid smiled at her and passed on the message.

"She may have a small sup of it," Susanna agreed.[10]

When the meal was over, Betty started to clear the table and Susanna rose. Samuel disappeared to his study and the children stood up.

"Today, Emilia, you will start your lessons. Betty, you must not disturb us and you must keep Sukey and Molly out of the schoolroom. Come children."

Sammy and Emilia followed their mother into the room she had set aside for herself and which would become known as the schoolroom. They sat down at the table and waited while Susanna got ready.

"Sammy, you will continue to read and learn the Book of Joshua. Emilia, you will learn the alphabet. Say after me …"

She followed the same pattern as she had with her son but Emilia was not quite as quick as he had been. Susanna had limitless patience and was a born teacher. She repeated the letters over and over again until Emilia could say them for herself. They stayed in the school room from nine o' clock until midday when they emerged to have their dinner, the main meal of the day. For this birthday dinner there was more meat and some soup. Betty had also baked a cake and laid out a little cheese. Emilia's eyes lit up. She loved cake and they did not often have it.

"May I have another piece?" she whispered.

Betty looked at Susanna who had heard. The mother nodded, smiling. Cakes were not a luxury they could often afford. The children were *never* allowed to eat between meals on pain of severest punishment.

---

10   Beer and ale was often consumed for breakfast in the early
      eighteenth century – even by children.

After dinner the children were sent to their bedrooms to rest and then at two o' clock Sammy and Emilia repaired to the schoolroom again. To Susanna's surprise her husband joined them.

"I should like to watch," he told her.

She nodded and continued to repeat the alphabet patiently to her daughter. Samuel did not share her patience and became restless. Eventually he could keep quiet no longer.

"I wonder at your patience!" he exclaimed. "You have told that child twenty times the same thing."

Susanna rebuked him calmly. "If I had satisfied myself by mentioning it only nineteen times, I should have lost all my labour. It was the twentieth time that crowned it."

She was right. By the end of the afternoon Emilia could recite her alphabet and was ready to start 'reading' the Book of Genesis the following day. The little girl was tired by the end of the day and her head started to nod. But she had to stay awake for family prayers which were always held at six o'clock in their father's study. She listened to his voice saying the familiar words but found it difficult to concentrate on them. When they were over, she was almost too tired to eat her supper of cold meat and cake left over from dinner.

"Betty, you may take Hetty and Mary up now," Susanna instructed when supper was over and Samuel had as usual disappeared.

The children went to bed about seven o'clock and Betty washed them, undressed them and put them to bed. She started with the youngest so when she had put the two babies to bed it was Emilia's turn.

"Don't forget to say your prayers, Emilia," her mother reminded her.

"No, Mama." Of course Emilia would not forget. As soon as she could speak, she had learnt to say the 'Lord's Prayer'.

She had been taught to say it when she got up and before she went to bed.

After Betty had undone her buttons and she was washed and in her night clothes she knelt by the bed and put her hands together. She said the 'Lord's Prayer' and then added a little prayer of her own to ask God to bless her parents, her baby sisters and her brother.

The next day after Emilia had said her alphabet, Susanna showed her the Book of Genesis as she had done with Samuel and by the end of the week, she, too, could recite some of the verses from memory.

When Sunday came, there was a break from lessons because Sunday was special. All the children were dressed in their best clothes and they walked across the fields to the church to hear their father preach. Little Hetty stayed at home with Betty.

"Remember to be quiet and listen," Susanna admonished them. She picked Molly up and carried her. The little deformed girl was a slow walker.

The church was cold but the children dared not show how uncomfortable they felt. They fixed their eyes on their father and tried to join in with the responses and the psalms. The rest of the day was spent quietly. Susanna read aloud from the Bible or from some improving book and the children sat in silence.

Susanna's views on educating her children were far in advance of her time. Although her method of learning by heart would be considered old-fashioned today, she recognised that not all children had the same ability to learn. Over thirty years later she wrote down her views in a letter to her famous son, John. [11]

A child should be taught what is necessary for it to know, as soon as that necessity exists, and the child is capable of learning. Among children there is a great disparity of

intellect, and in the power of apprehension and compre-
hension ... When a child is capable of learning any thing,
give that teaching; but let the teaching be regularly
graduated; let it go on from step to step never obliging it
to learn what it cannot yet comprehend.

She went on to explain her method of teaching:

We begin very properly with letters, or the elementary
signs of language; teach the child to distinguish them
from each other and give them in their names some
notion of their power. We then teach them to combine
them into simple syllables; syllables into words; words
into sentences; sentences into speeches, or regular discourse.

She then added a shrewd comment as applicable now as it
was then:

A child must understand what it is doing, before it can do
what it ought ... Few are taught to *spell* their mother
tongue correctly.

She referred scathingly to:

some original letters of lords and ladies ... where the
writing is elegant, and the spelling execrable.

Susanna liked order and she applied 'method' to everything
she did. To manage such a large household with so little
money and with a husband who was of little practical help
to her, required great organisation. Susanna laid down rules
for her family which had to be obeyed.

The children had to go to bed at set times, get up when
they were told, dress themselves as soon as they were able
and change into clean linen regularly. When they were
small, they had to sleep for 'three hours in the morning and

---

11   July 24th 1732 — Adam Clarke, *Memoirs of the Wesley Family*.

three hours in the afternoon; afterwards two hours till they need none at all.'

Susanna could not bear to hear 'that most odious noise of the crying of children' and it 'was rarely heard in the house'. This was because 'when turned a year old, (the children) were taught to fear the rod and to cry softly, by which means they escaped abundance of correction which they might otherwise have had.' She felt that 'in order to form the minds of the children, the first thing to be done is to conquer their will, and bring them to an obedient temper ... When the will of a child is totally subdued, and it is brought to revere and stand in awe of the parents, then a great many childish follies ... may be passed by.' [12]

Susanna's discipline was superb for she only had to hold up a finger at her erring offspring for the child immediately to behave itself. She therefore used the rod rarely although her husband was not so forbearing and beat his sons regularly to Susanna's distress. By twentieth century standards her methods were harsh but she was in fact an enlightened parent and none of her children suffered from their upbringing. They all remained very close to their mother and regarded her with great affection. They were not cowed by her 'method' and were encouraged to think for themselves and to discuss freely as their mother had done in her father's house.

Susanna was becoming increasingly concerned about her eldest son. "Mr Holland is a very strange man, I have heard," she told her husband. "Sammy is not happy at his school. Indeed he tells me he learns little."

Samuel frowned. He too had heard rumours of the eccentric behaviour of the headmaster. He had no doubt that

---

12   Adam Clarke, Op. cit.

excessive drinking was to blame. "You think we should remove him, Sukey?"

"I do. He can join in my lessons with the other children and who better to teach him the classics than yourself."

"Perhaps you are right. Very well. I will speak to Mr Holland this afternoon."

Sammy had been at the school for only a year and he had learned little there. He was delighted to be back and join in lessons with his sisters and then have his father's undivided attention.

As well as teaching her children the three 'Rs', Susanna did not neglect their spiritual training. This she considered the most important thing. As soon as they could speak, they were taught to pray morning and evening; the Bible was the most important book in the house and all her children knew the Scriptures very thoroughly.

Their father, too, played some part in their education. He was recognised as an excellent classical scholar and he enjoyed imparting his knowledge to his eldest son who absorbed it greedily. Samuel knew that a classical education was vital for a boy who would need it to obtain a place in a good school. He and his wife were determined that Sammy would have as good an education as they could manage.

But Samuel did not neglect his daughters and they, too, were taught Latin and Greek. Hetty, as well as being beautiful, proved to be one of the brightest of the girls. Her father was very proud of her quick mind and spent a great deal of time teaching her. He was delighted when she was able to read the New Testament in Greek when she was only eight years old.

However she did not quite fit the mould expected of young ladies in the eighteenth century. She was too lively and she often rebelled against the strict regime at Epworth, causing her parents great anxiety.

However, when the Wesley children became targets of verbal abuse from the villagers, Hetty was quite capable of retaliating in kind. She never lacked courage. Unfortunately the villagers did not stop at verbal attack. One night the doors and windows seemed to be rattling in the wind more than usual. When Susanna went to inspect the front door, she discovered that the hinge had been loosened so the door collapsed when she touched it. No wind could have done that and she shuddered as she wondered whether the villagers' next move would be to invade the house. The fen folk might have no book learning but they were skilful with their hands. Samuel mended the door but after that it did not fit properly and there was always a draught blowing throughout. That was not the only damage caused. Susanna had been delighted to find that there was the remains of a flax crop on one of the fields and she carefully tended this so that she could sell it to make a little money. She was devastated one morning to discover that during the night the crop had been burnt by a malicious hand.

"Why are they so cruel to us?" she cried. "What have we done to them?"

Samuel put his arm round her. "They are still God's children," he reminded her. "We must forgive them."

It was easy for him to say that, Susanna reflected. He didn't have to feed and clothe the children. As if reading her mind, he handed her three gold sovereigns.

"Where did these come from?" she asked suspiciously.

"Never mind, Sukey. Just use it for what you need."

She was sure he was borrowing money and adding to their debt but she was too tired to argue. The money was soon spent and it was not long before she was again with child. Clumsy and very near her time, she made her way to her husband's study.

"Samuel, I must have money to buy coals. The children will die of the cold." Her tone was desperate.

Samuel peered at her over his book. It was obvious to her he was still on a higher plane. He had no idea what it was like to live in the real world. It took him some time to descend to her level and meanwhile her irritation increased.

"Samuel, what are we to do?"

"There is some money in the box over there. Take it, my love, and pray do not interrupt me again. I have work to do." He picked up his pen and started to write.

Muttering to herself, Susanna flounced over to the box and opened it. She sighed with relief to find the gleam of silver inside. Six shillings should buy some coal and perhaps a little more flour. She cast her husband an exasperated glance and left the room. At least the cold could be lessened for a short while.

The next day Susanna's pains started and she produced, with the help of the hastily summoned midwife, twin sons who were tiny and sadly did not survive.

"Oh God," she cried in her despair. "Why do you punish me? Am I not to bear another living child?"

It began to look as though she were right. By the turn of the century, she'd lost two more little boys. She'd borne eleven children of whom five had died. She was weary of childbearing but it seemed she had to bear it even if the children did not survive. Was this not why God had ordained marriage between a man and a woman?

During the first year of the new century, Susanna decided that two hours out of each precious twenty four hours must be set aside for her private devotions. On the stroke of seven in the evening as the children were starting to go to bed, she would go to her room and kneel down at her prayer chair.[13] There she would pray and commune with God. She kept a journal in which she pondered on the nature of God, what

He had done for her and how she could improve the quality of her spiritual life. Her entries show how close she was to her Maker and how much she relied on His help in the day to day running of her home.

One Sunday she wrote, 'Oh most happy day. Lord I can never sufficiently adore this infinite love and goodness in appropriating this seventh part of my time to thee. May these moments ever be employed in thy service.'

Another Sunday entry read, 'Blessed be God for bringing me to another of his own most happy days.'

This was followed by a joyful comment on the Monday. 'Another blessed day. Lord how could we support the cares and pains of life were it not for the refreshment of thy dear and Holy day?'[14]

---

13   This had a drawer for her Bible and the back could be drawn forward to provide a table on which to rest the Book (see plate section).

14   The Headingley Mss. Wesley College, Bristol

CHAPTER FOUR

Imprisoned For Debt!

Before the century was a year old Susanna had given birth to twins. When they too died, she became very depressed but she was powerless to prevent yet another pregnancy. She was becoming increasingly irritated with her husband who took his pleasure and then left her to run the household as best she could. It was she who worried and scrimped and saved; he was too busy with his writing.

He had recently published a short discourse on baptism. In spite of his disapproval of the lifestyle of his former patron, the Marquis of Normanby, he had remained on good terms with the Marquis and his wife; he had even retained the nominal position of Lord Castleton's Chaplain. In the front of his latest work he described himself as 'Chaplain to the most Honourable John, Lord Marquis of Normanby'.

The following year he dedicated his 'History of the Old and New Testaments' to the Marquis's wife. Soon after this he came into the kitchen where Susanna was at work exclaiming, "Sukey, I have just received twenty guineas from the Marquis and five guineas from the Marchioness. Are they not good to us?"

"Very good, husband," agreed his wife. "They are kind in spite of the way they live."

Like the dutiful wife she was, Susanna tried hard in the face of increasing difficulties. But even she had her breaking point and it came one cold March evening in 1702 during family prayers.

Samuel had just said his customary prayer for King William. He waited for the 'Amen' which he should have heard from Susanna but it did not come. Quivering with rage, he leapt to his feet and ordered her to follow him to his study. Once there, he glared at her.

"Sukey," he bellowed, "why did you not say 'Amen' to the prayer for the king?"

Susanna was taken aback. She had never said 'Amen' to this particular prayer so why was he upset?

"Because," she replied calmly, "I do not believe the Prince of Orange to be the rightful King."

Samuel became almost apoplectic with rage. His tiny five foot figure shook. Susanna frowned. This promised to be worse than any disagreement they had yet had.

Clenching his fist, Samuel snarled, "If that be the case, you and I must part, Madam; for if we have two Kings, we must have two beds." He knelt beside his desk. "I call divine vengeance upon myself and all my descendants if I ever touch you or go to bed with you again unless you beg God's pardon and mine for not saying 'Amen' to the prayer for the King."

He flung himself out of the room ignoring his wife's steady stare. Susanna did not move. A little later, she heard the front door slam and soon afterwards, horses' hooves clattered outside the house. The sound faded away into the distance. No doubt her angry husband had gone to London. He was a representative of the Diocese of Lincoln on the Convocation, a church assembly which met in London several times a year.

His accepting the office of a member of Convocation had put a further strain upon their marriage as it cost him fifty pounds a year. With a growing family, he could ill afford this fee and Susanna was not the only one who criticised him for taking it on in spite of his limited resources.

He had never left her in anger before and she felt a cold chill upon her. Had she been wrong? But he had been just as stubborn as she had. Dragging herself upstairs, she shut herself in her study and stared unseeingly out of the window. All was quiet. What the children were doing she did not know and at that moment she did not care. Annoyed though she had been with her husband, she still loved him and she was upset at the manner of his leaving.

Samuel did not return and she was unhappy for several days. There was no one to talk to about her distress so at last she decided she had to write to someone. Her choice was Lady Yarborough, a neighbour, with whom she had become friendly. She knew this lady would be sympathetic as, like Susanna, she had supported the clergy who had refused to take the Oath of Allegiance to William and Mary. She wrote on March 7th,

> I'm almost ashamed to own what extreme disturbance this accident has given me. I am inexpressibly miserable, for I can see no possibility of reconciling these differences, though I would submit to anything in the world to oblige him to live in the house with me.[15]

The day after Susanna wrote her letter, the King died and Queen Anne, the younger daughter of James II, ascended the throne. As Susanna accepted this lady's claim to the

---

15   *Proceedings of the Wesley Historical Society:* taken from *Susanna Wesley and the Puritan Tradition in Methodism* by John Newton.

throne, she hoped that the differences with her husband might be forgotten. But it was not to be. Samuel had not forgiven his wife and she had not apologised. On March 15th she again wrote to Lady Yarborough.

> I've represented as long as I could be heard the sin of the Oath and all consequences of it to my husband but he cannot be convinced he has done ill nor does (the King's death) make any alteration in his mind. [16]

It was not only Samuel's stubbornness that concerned his wife. He returned to the Rectory but he kept his oath and had little to do with her. They talked little and the tension between them was growing. One evening he requested her to go to his study and when she was seated, he dropped his bombshell. Wandering restlessly round the room, he avoided her eyes.

"At Easter, I am for London again, Sukey," he told her.

His frequent trips to London were no surprise to her and she merely nodded. It would even be a relief to be free again of him for a while but she was not prepared for his next announcement.

"I have a longing to return to sea. I intend to try if I can get a Chaplain's place in a Man of War."

Susanna gasped. He might make her angry but he was still her husband. How would she cope without him?

"But Samuel, what about the children? I have six little ones. How will they survive?"

"I will take good care of them," he assured her.

---

16   *Proceedings of the Wesley Historical Society:* taken from
      Susanna Wesley and the Puritan Tradition in Methodism by
      John Newton.

"But how ..." Susanna compressed her lips. How could she tackle him now about his debts, his frequent absences and the little time he spent with his children? She sometimes wondered if he knew them at all. She changed the subject.

"Our disagreement is not resolved, Samuel. Can we not each seek the judgement of those wiser than we are to resolve our dispute?"

"You know I am prepared to refer the whole to the Archbishop of York and the Bishop of Lincoln. If you will not be determined by them, I will do anything rather than live with a person who is the declared enemy of my country."

"But before them I will be condemned without a fair hearing. I see no reason for asking either your pardon or God Almighty's for what I believe to be right."

"You are too obstinate and proud, Sukey. You have done me great injury."

"But I have only held to what I believe to be the truth," she cried. "Since I'm willing to let you quietly enjoy your opinions, you ought not to deprive me of my little liberty of conscience."

"While I am in London, you will have time to consider what to do — whether you will submit to my judgement and implicitly obey me in all matters of conscience."

"I cannot do so in this case, Samuel."

"Then we must part. I have nothing more to say on the matter."

Her respect was rapidly dwindling but she knew she would gain nothing by arguing further. He was as inflexible as she was. She sighed as she left the room. A few days later on April 5th Samuel left for London.

Susanna was philosophical and accepted his departure with resignation. She wrote again to Lady Yarborough. 'I'm more easy in the thought of parting because I think we are not likely to live happily together … Yet if anything should befall him at sea, we should be in no very good condition.'[17]

In her indomitable way Susanna coped without her husband. She continued to go about her duties. She could not neglect them because she was having an argument with her husband. The children still had to be taught, their clothes washed, the food cooked and the house kept in order. There was very little money and by the end of the day Susanna was almost too tired to think about her obstinate husband. Her next baby was also due.

But the cause of their disagreement still rankled. Lady Yarborough advised her to put her case to the outstanding cleric, Dr George Hicks, who had been one of the first to reject the claims of William of Orange.

Soon after her husband left, Susanna wrote to him outlining her case. She knew that by now her husband would have put *his* case to *his* chosen supporters. Dr Hicks, as she had expected, supported her without reservation. He considered 'it was perjury' for Samuel to make an oath which prevented him from sleeping with his wife. It did not accord with his marriage vows, he told her and it would be 'a continuance of perjury for him to persist in the performance of it.' He even suggested she should appeal to the Archbishop of York and the Bishop of Lincoln and ask them to persuade her husband to change his mind.

He concluded, 'Wherefore good Madam, stick to God and your conscience which are your best friends, whatever you may suffer for adhering to them.'

Susanna was greatly relieved to have the support of such a man as Dr Hicks. She replied that his letter 'gave (her) the greatest satisfaction of anything in (her) whole life.'

---

17   Ibid. (Same source).

Before she could follow his advice and write to the Archbishop of York and the Bishop of Lincoln, Samuel returned. He was in a chastened mood. Susanna was wary of his change of mood until he told her what had happened. As he rode away in a furious temper, he had met a clergyman who had ridden with him for part of the way. Realising that Samuel was unhappy, his companion persuaded him to unburden himself.

"He said that you were to be condemned for not submitting to my judgement, Sukey," he told her. "But then he said I was wrong to leave you. He said you needed my support — particularly now." He glanced down at her swollen stomach. "And I suddenly realised he was right. I should not have left you. So I've come back."

Susanna was silent. He had not apologised and neither had he accepted her right to have her own opinions. But she was glad to have him back. She held out her hands to her husband.

"Welcome home, Samuel," she said.

Disaster had not yet forsaken the Wesleys. One day at the end of July 1702 Samuel was visiting a sick parishioner and Susanna and the children were together in Samuel's study. Susanna was teaching them and suddenly Emilia interrupted.

"Mama, I can smell smoke."

Susanna frowned. She did not encourage interruptions but she knew the danger of fire and she stopped. Molly started to cry quietly but stopped as her mother quelled her with a look.

"Stay here, children. I will see what it is."

She opened the door and smoke poured in. Coughing and gasping, she shut it again.

"Sammy—bring Molly. Emilia and Sukey—follow me."

Grabbing hold of Molly and Hetty, the youngest, she opened the door and staggered through it, coughing and spluttering. Reaching the outside, she collapsed with the children on the ground. She was very near her time and she was exhausted.

"Sukey didn't come, Mama." She heard Emilia wail and started to get up.

"You lie there, Mistress. We'll get her out," said a gruff voice.

Neighbours from nearby farms had appeared and the man who had spoken dashed into the smoke, reappearing moments later with the unconscious Sukey in his arms. Susanna shut her eyes and left Emilia to tend her younger sister. She didn't want to watch her home burn.

"What has happened?" Horses' hooves beat on the ground near her and her husband's white face loomed over her. "The children?"

"All safe," she croaked.

"Thank God." He disappeared and joined his neighbours in their efforts to halt the fire and save their belongings. Books and furniture were piling up around her.

"Come, Sukey." She felt gentle hands lifting her. "We are safe now and we have not lost many of our goods. My books are safe."

That would, of course, be his prime concern, she thought wryly as she was led into the ruined Rectory. As he sat her down on one of the remaining chairs, she looked sadly at him.

"This is the finger of God pointing at us, Samuel. Has he punished us for our folly?"

Samuel looked ashamed. "Perhaps he has, Sukey, but let us thank him that all our children are safe."

"Amen," said his wife fervently.

Two thirds of the Rectory had been destroyed and until it was rebuilt, they had to live in very cramped conditions. Susanna coped with her usual serenity and soon afterwards baby Anne was born. As usual the baby was delivered by a midwife but Susanna was not very well for some time following the birth and so did not attend the baptism. She was however, able to attend the service in the Parish Church for 'The Churching of Women'. In Susanna's case it was becoming an annual event!

Soberly dressed in a dark dress with a matching bonnet she presented her fee of sixpence and the white chrisom, the linen cloth in which baby Anne had been baptised. Sometimes cash to the value of the cloth was paid instead of presenting the chrisom to the church. However Susanna could barely afford the fee for the 'Churching' so it was logical for her to give instead the chrisom to the Church. Having paid her dues, she knelt down to hear her husband in his role as priest say, "Forasmuch as it has pleased Almighty God of his goodness to give you safe deliverance and has preserved you in the great danger of childbirth; you shall therefore give hearty thanks unto God … "

Susanna's lips formed the word 'Amen'. She was indeed thankful that God had once again allowed her child to live. Bowing her head, she listened to her husband read the hundredth and sixteenth Psalm; then she said the Lord's Prayer and made the appropriate responses. There was no Communion on this occasion and at the end of the service, Susanna struggled to her feet. She still felt very weak but would not admit it.

Since his return, Samuel had been very affectionate to her. He had apparently revoked his vow of never sharing her bed again and it was not long before she was again pregnant. She accepted it with her usual calm but sometimes she wished she did not get pregnant so easily. It made her so tired.

Her baby son was born on 17th June 1703 and christened John Benjamin. There was always a very close link between Susanna and this son who was born of the reconciliation between her and her husband. John, too, was always very close to his mother and her influence can be seen very clearly in the way the ministry of this famous preacher later progressed.

Like his elder brother, he also would have to receive a formal education. In 1704 when Sammy was fourteen, he was sent to Westminster School. Samuel and Susanna had saved desperately to give their eldest son a chance in life but when the time came for him to leave, Susanna was heartbroken. He was the first of her fledglings to leave the nest but for the rest of his life he would be pursued by his mother's letters and instructions. He accepted this gracefully and always remained very close to her.

The situation in the village did not improve. Samuel was still unpopular . Many of his parishioners sympathised with the Dissenters' views and preferred simple services. Samuel, who had once been a Dissenter, had renounced those views and now adhered to the formality of the Church of England, the established church. He did not hesitate to denounce the Dissenters from the pulpit and publish pamphlets against them. This did nothing to endear him to his congregation who made life as difficult as they could for him and his family. He complicated things even more by borrowing money from his enemies and thus putting himself in their power. Susanna was aware of this and had tried remonstrating with him but he would not listen. She reflected sadly that, in spite of their reconciliation, they rarely agreed on anything nowadays. The halcyon period of their 'second honeymoon' had not lasted long but nevertheless she still loved her husband and had respect for him.

Things came to a head in the elections of 1705. The current members were Sir John Thorold and Mr Dymoke.

Both were Tories and supported the High Church position. The opposing Whig candidates were Colonel Whichcott and Mr Bertie, both of whom were Dissenters. Samuel was canvassed by both parties and, at first, foolishly agreed to vote for one from each side. He chose Sir John and the Colonel. However when Whichcott started attacking the High Church position and insulting all who did not hold the Dissenting viewpoint, he changed his mind and announced he would only vote for the Tories. This infuriated his parishioners, most of whom were Dissenters.

As he left the church on the Sunday after announcing his decision, one of them, Robert Darwin, shouted at him, "You are a rascal and scoundrel. We will turn you out."

The cry was taken up by others and they followed him to the Rectory, taunting him all the way. When they saw the children in the yard, they shouted at them too. Samuel hustled them inside and slammed the door while the mob howled outside and banged on it.

"I cannot vote for a man who is insulting my Church and abusing the memory of the late king whom I regard as a martyr,"[18] Samuel shouted above the noise. "I will vote only for the friends of the Church."

"Yes, dear," said Susanna weakly as she tried to calm the children. Three weeks before this, she had given birth to another son and she was still very weak.

When the noise had finally died down, Samuel looked thoughtful. "You are tired, my dear," he said to his wife. "Joan can take the child across the road tonight to give you some rest. I have to go to Lincoln to cast my vote."

---

18   Charles I

"Is it safe, Samuel?" asked Susanna anxiously. "You know how they hate you for changing your position."

"God will protect me. I have as much right to vote as I please as any other freeholder."

It was Tuesday 29th May 1705. Susanna was relieved to let the nurse take the new baby and looked forward to a peaceful night. She was not to have one. That evening the Epworth men descended on the Rectory again. All night long they kept up a raucous row outside it. Susanna, still weak from childbirth, lay cringing as she heard the ribald jests about her husband; her head throbbed from the incessant drumming and she found it impossible to sleep. Were these the same men who had helped to save her family during the fire? It was difficult to believe.

Suddenly above the cacophony sounded the most blood curdling blast of all. It was the bellowing of the ram's horn. This, she remembered, had brought down the walls of Jericho and, as she covered her ears to try to blot out the hideous sound, she wondered if it would also bring down the walls of the Epworth Rectory. How long would they keep it up? Not for the first time she wished Samuel had been a little more conciliatory.

The children would be trembling in their beds but she was too exhausted to go to them. When she heard the crack of pistol shots, she hardly reacted. Pulling the covers over her head, she tried to sleep but it was hopeless. The noise continued all night and it seemed to get louder. Desperately she prayed for relief but on this occasion her God seemed so far away. She took some deep breaths. She must be calm. At least the house had withstood the blowing of the ram's horn and was still standing.

Trying to shut out the racket, she reflected on her father. He too, had been a Dissenter like many of those now shouting abuse outside her house. But he had been a gentleman and would never have resorted to the brutish behaviour of her present tormentors. He had also suffered persecution at the hands of the Establishment for his beliefs; but although he had sometimes attacked from the pulpit those who disagreed with him, he never showed Samuel's lack of tact and even those who had rejected his views had respected him. Susanna loved her fiery little husband but she did wish he would show a little more tolerance towards those with whom he disagreed. Still thinking of the two men in her life, she dozed.

It seemed no time before a new disturbance roused her. The noise outside the house had ceased but now inside the house she could hear voices shouting, wailing and crying. Opening her eyes, she started to sit up. She must go down to see what the noise was all about.

Before she could get out of bed, the door burst open and Betty, the maid, rushed into the room carrying a white bundle. Crying and screaming, she thrust it into Susanna's arms. "Oh ma'am, the nurse overlaid it when she slept. She said she hardly slept because of the noise but she must have done because she laid on the child and smothered it and oh ma'am what are we to do? And the master away and—oh … oh … !"

Susanna had hardly listened to the tirade. With horror, she looked down at the tiny dead face peeping out from the swaddling clothes. Gently she touched the cold cheeks of the son to whom she had given birth but three weeks earlier. Tears pricked her eyes. He had lived but now he was dead because of a raucous mob.

As if her thoughts had conjured them up, the noise started again and she winced. The little maid was still crouched on the floor and now she started to wail again in competition with the persistent drumming outside. Susanna cast an exasperated glance at her. Her own tears had stopped and there were things to do.

"Betty, stop crying. Betty." She had to shout to make herself heard. Startled, the maid looked up. "Take the child and send Robin to tell Mrs Japes to come here."

Trembling, the little maid did as she was told and Susanna prepared for the sad day ahead. Her husband had still not returned and she supposed him to be still in Lincoln. Mrs Japes, the midwife who had attended the birth, prepared the child for burial. She wrapped it in the chrisom, the fine linen cloth in which the child had been wrapped at its recent baptism. Custom decreed that the chrisom should act as a winding sheet if the child died within a month of baptism. With the grieving mother, the midwife arranged the burial herself so before Samuel returned, the little one had been interred in the earth.

Samuel returned later that evening and hearing of his return, the mob returned. The children were in the yard but terrified, they rushed indoors to avoid the taunting.

"They said they would turn us out so that we would have to beg," a white faced Emilia told her father.

"They called us devils," piped up Sukey. "We're not devils, are we, Papa?"

"Of course you are not, my child," Samuel comforted them.

"I am glad you are not hurt, Samuel," said Susanna. "God preserved you."

"When I entered the castle yard in Lincoln, I was met by a clergyman friendly to me. He said the men of Epworth intended to do me a mischief. 'They will squeeze your guts out if they catch you in the castle yard—those were their very words,' he told me. I knew it was not safe so I returned home by way of Gainsborough."

Epworth was becoming so uncomfortable that when he was offered the position of Chaplain to Colonel Lepelle's

Regiment, he decided to accept it. Surely anything must be better than Epworth.

"The regiment is to be based in England," he told Susanna. "It is through the good offices of the Duke of Marlborough, it has been offered to me. He was very pleased with the work I wrote about his life."[19]

Samuel went to London but he was doomed to disappointment. The offer was withdrawn and he returned, discouraged, to Epworth.

"It seems that my enemies have again been successful in damaging my prospects," he told his wife. "God must wish us to stay here. Let us hope things will improve."

They did not! Barely a month after the election fiasco, disaster once again struck the Wesleys. One afternoon, when Samuel emerged from the church after christening a child, he was arrested for debt.

"You owe Mr Pinder the sum of thirty pounds," he was told. "You must immediately pay the whole sum or go to prison."

Samuel knew Mr Pinder was a friend of Colonel Whichcott, the Whig candidate in the recent elections. No doubt they had plotted against him. He would not be forgiven for supporting the wrong candidate.

The Rector drew himself up to his full five feet. "You know very well I have no money. You have burnt my flax so I have lost the revenue from that and I have to rebuild my house and feed my children. How can I pay you what I don't possess?"

"Then you must go to prison."

---

19   In 1705 he had written a Eulogy of Marlborough. Taken from *The Life and Times of Samuel Wesley* by Luke Tyerman.

Samuel knew there was no alternative but he grieved for his family. How would they manage while he was shut up in the debtors' prison in Lincoln Castle? Susanna bore this latest misfortune with her usual calm but she had no idea how she was going to feed her family on ten shillings which was all she possessed. They would have to live only on bread and milk until things improved. Samuel had been foolish to borrow money from those who had no love for him but it was not his fault that a Rector's stipend was not sufficient to feed a growing family. What could she do to help him?

The children were in the yard and she was alone in the kitchen. Pulling off her rings, she wrapped them in a piece of cloth so she could send them to Samuel to ease his life. When he received them, he was touched by the love shown him by the wife whom he had promised to 'love and cherish'. He knew how much she valued her rings which were almost all she had to remind her of her old life. He sent them back to her. He could not bring himself to pawn them.

The following day when Susanna went to unlock the door, she realised it was already unlocked. One wooden panel had been smashed and the lock drawn back. She had heard their dog barking in the night. No doubt he had prevented the intruders entering. More problems faced her as she went to milk the cows. Three of them had been stabbed! The poor beasts were in agony and she did what she could to ease their pain. Whether the intention had been to kill, she did not know but there would certainly be no milk for some time. How was she to feed the children?

It was obvious a sword had done the deed. One wound was very deep and Susanna was surprised it had missed the animal's heart. How long would it take them to heal?

From prison Samuel wrote to Archbishop Sharp of York explaining his situation and the concern he had for his children. His debts, he said, amounted to about three hundred pounds — a considerable sum in those days. Samuel's annual stipend from the church was only two hundred pounds, which he would supplement by selling flax from his crop. He usually received a good price for this but, as he told the Archbishop, some malicious miscreants had burnt his crop and so he had lost half of his revenue. His house also needed rebuilding and his cows had been stabbed, depriving them of milk.

Archbishop Sharp was not proof against this cry from the heart. He had already contributed some money after the fire to assist in the rebuilding of the Rectory and had paid some of Samuel's debts. Because of his influence, others too had come to the rescue.

However, on this occasion the Archbishop decided to play a more active role. One fine Autumn morning Susanna was interrupted while she was teaching the children by a knocking at the door. This was immediately followed by a hurried knock at her own door and Betty burst in before she had been bidden to enter.

Susanna, who made it a strict rule that she was never to be interrupted during school hours, frowned as she looked up.

"Oh ma'am, the Archbishop's here," Betty gasped.

Susanna stood up. "Straighten your cap, Betty, and calm down. Go down and let his Grace in and tell him I will be with him directly."

The maid dropped a curtsey and disappeared. Susanna replaced a hair pin that had dropped out and smoothed her apron. "Children, you will continue with your work. When I return, you will repeat to me what you have done."

Calmly, she made her way to the kitchen. She knew the Archbishop to be kind-hearted and in her father's house she had met some of the leading clergymen of the day. She hoped her visitor would be able to help her poverty-stricken family.

He was standing beside the kitchen table when she entered, looking at the smoke blackened walls.

"Good morning, Mrs Wesley. I am so sorry to hear of your misfortunes."

Susanna dropped a curtsey. "Thank you, your Grace. We are honoured by your visit. Pray sit down."

He did so on one side of the table and Susanna sat opposite him. She should offer him some refreshment but she had nothing suitable and she hoped he understood. She folded her hands in her lap and waited for him to speak.

"Your husband wrote to me telling me what has befallen you. He is concerned, he tells me, that he has to leave his poor lambs in the midst of so many wolves. But he says you bear your difficulties with the courage which he always expects from you."

Susanna looked down, slightly embarrassed. "I try to, your Grace."

"He is doing great work in the prison, Mrs Wesley. He looks on it as his parish. He reads prayers twice a day and preaches every Sunday afternoon. He told me he has also written to the Society for Propagating Christian Knowledge to ask for some books that he can distribute among his fellow prisoners."

"He is always zealous to serve his God," Susanna said smiling.

"Indeed he is, Mrs Wesley. I know he does not like to beg but now that he is in prison, life must be very difficult for you."

"Yes, my Lord, it is."

"Tell me, Mrs Wesley, whether you have ever really not had bread when you needed it."

Susanna looked up at him. "My Lord," she replied. "I will freely own that, strictly speaking, I never suffered from the lack of bread. But it was often so difficult to get it and so hard to pay for it afterwards, that it sometimes tasted very unpleasant. To have bread on such terms is almost as wretched as having none at all."

The Archbishop nodded. "I can understand your sentiments, Mrs Wesley and I hope I can ease your situation. I will pay your husband's debts and will try to relieve your present difficulties. Now I must go." He stood up and moved towards the door.

Susanna followed him. "It was very kind of your Grace to spend time to visit me. I am very appreciative of your help as I know my husband is too."

"Good-bye, my dear Mrs Wesley. Keep close to God who is always there in time of trouble."

"I will, your Grace. Thank you."

Watching him ride off, her heart was full of thankfulness to God for his grace. Kneeling down by the kitchen table, she thanked him for his goodness and for the kindness of his servant, Archbishop Sharp. It was not until she rose from her knees that she realised a number of golden sovereigns lay on the table top. She had not seen him place them there but as she counted them and carried them to a safe place, she knew that for a time at least her monetary problems were solved.

Soon after Samuel returned home, Susanna became pregnant again. On 8th May 1706 she gave birth to another daughter, Martha, affectionately known as 'Patty'. The following year on 18th December their last son was born. He was named Charles.

During this month also one of their enemies had a very unpleasant accident. Robert Darwin, one of the richest men in Epworth, was one of the most implacable of Samuel's enemies. He had taunted the Rector in his misfortunes, was always in the forefront of any attacks on the Wesleys, verbally abused Susanna and the children and had done all he could to bring about Samuel's ruin.

The man had become drunk at a local fair and as he rode home down the hill, his horse fell, pitching him face down on the ground. His face was torn, his nose broken, one eye damaged and his neck dislocated. He never spoke again and died the following day.

"It is one of the most dreadful examples of God's justice that I have known," remarked Susanna when she heard the news. "This man has been cut off in the midst of his sins."[20]

"He has certainly been punished severely," agreed Samuel who had been released from prison some weeks earlier. He smiled at his wife. What a comfort she was to him. What would he do without her? He might on occasion take her for granted and not show her the affection she deserved but he had a deep regard for her. In September 1706, he wrote a moving letter to his eldest son.

> You know what you owe to the best of mothers ... Often reflect on the tender and peculiar love which your dear mother has always expressed towards you. (Remember) the particular care she took of your education when she struggled with so many pains and infirmities; and, above all, the wholesome and motherly advice and counsel which she has often given you.' He continued, 'These obligations ... must last to the very close of life. You will not forget to evidence this by supporting and comforting her in her (old) age.[21]

---

20 *The Life and Times of Samuel Wesley* by Luke Tyerman.

21 This appeared in the *Methodist Magazine* of 1846. Taken from *The Life and Times of Samuel Wesley* by Luke Tyerman.

CHAPTER FIVE

Fire At Epworth Rectory

It was February 9th 1709. Because Susanna was very near her time, Samuel was sleeping in another room while Emilia and Sukey had moved in with their mother. Susanna felt very weary; as she ponderously climbed the stairs to go to bed, she hoped that her vague husband would remember to check that the bags of meal in the corn room were still safe before he locked up the Rectory for the night. The children were asleep and as usual a cold north east wind was blowing across the fens and making the doors and windows rattle.

Samuel was unaware of this as he sat in his study wrestling with his latest poem eulogising his hero, the Duke of Marlborough. One line still escaped him. Sighing, he decided to go to bed and hope his subconscious would provide the missing rhyme while he slept.

In a trance, he picked up his candle and left the room. About to go to the front door to lock it, he remembered his wife's instructions and, still meditating on the elusive rhyme, he headed for the corn room. Holding his candle aloft, he counted the sacks. All were apparently correct and, unaware that the flame of his candle had left a spark in the thatch above his head, he locked the front door and retired to bed.

A little later, the household was aroused by shrieks from twelve year old Hetty who slept in a small room under the eaves.

"Help! Help! Fire! Fire! My bed's alight. Fire's fallen from the roof on it."

Samuel heard the shout of "fire" outside his window as well. Leaping out of bed, clad only in his night-shirt, he grabbed his breeches trying unsuccessfully to pull them on as he rushed into Susanna's room.

"Sukey, Sukey. Hurry, the house is on fire. Emilia, Sukey, wake up. Hurry."

Susanna clasped her wrapping gown[22] about her. Then, careful as always, she headed for the little chest where she kept her household money. She had hoarded twenty guineas in gold and silver to pay some of their debts. Samuel grabbed her arm.

"Come, Sukey. There's no time. Fly for your life. Take the girls."

She obeyed him while Samuel burst open the door of the nursery where the other five children slept in two beds.

"Nurse, bring the children down. The house is on fire. Hurry."

Coughing and spluttering, Joan, the nurse, scooped up two year old Charles into her arms. She shook the other children awake.

---

22   The wrapping gown was probably the forerunner of the dressing gown. It was a loose overlapping gown fastened round the waist with a girdle.

"Follow me, children," she screamed, leading the way down the stairs through clouds of smoke. Susanna and Samuel followed them and their three older daughters to the smoke filled hall.

"Unlock the door, Samuel. Hurry." Susanna coughed as she breathed in the acrid smoke. She hurriedly put her hand over her nose and mouth. "Children cover your faces."

"I left the key upstairs," Samuel gasped, turning to rush up the stairs. Holding his breeches over his face, he cut a ridiculous figure but no one had time to dwell on that.

"Samuel, do be careful," moaned Susanna.

The smoke had blown out some of the windows and Joan herded the children towards them.

"Jump out," she commanded.

"The garden door's open," shrieked Emilia. "Hetty and Sukey follow me. Mama, can you come?"

"I will wait for your father."

Emilia, Sukey and Hetty disappeared and the rest of the children jumped through the windows as Samuel forced his way back through the blazing stairs and opened the front door. The ever present wind rushed in and fanned the already destructive fire. Susanna, unable—because of her condition—to jump through the window or force her way through the flames to the garden door, struggled through the flames to the front door and collapsed on the ground outside. She could not believe that her home was on fire for the second time. Her lips were blackened and her face was covered in soot. She was unrecognisable but, apart from her burnt legs which were very sore, she was not badly hurt. She was too exhausted to move; the crackle and hiss of the flames assailed her senses and she tried, unsuccessfully, to cover her ears.

There was such confusion everywhere that for a while it was difficult to ascertain whether all the family were safe.

"John," screamed Susanna, suddenly realising that the six-year-old was not with them.

"Oh ma'am, I shouted at him to wake up and follow me," Joan wailed.

"There he is, Mama!" exclaimed Emilia pointing to the upper window through which could be seen a small terrified face.

Samuel rushed towards the door but the flames beat him back. Tears streaming down his face, he knelt down to pray for the soul of his lost son. But John was not lost.

Although some of the villagers could be seen smirking at the downfall of their detested Rector, others could not stand by and watch a child die.

"Let's get him," shouted a big burly fellow pushing through the crowds. "Jake, climb on my shoulders."

Jake, a small wiry man, did as he was told but his hold was precarious and he fell. Picking himself up, he climbed up again and this time managed to reach the child and drag him out of the window.

There was a collective sigh of relief as John was rescued. Just moments later, the sighs turned to gasps as the crowd heard an ominous crack of breaking timbers and watched the whole roof collapse into the remains of the building .

"Oh my son, my son, thank God." For once in her life, Susanna gave way to tears as she embraced the little smoke blackened figure who clung desperately to her. "I will take particular care of this child whom God has mercifully spared. He is indeed a brand plucked from the burning." She looked at the charred remains of their home and then at her husband who was leaning over her. She could think of only one thing to say.

"Are your books safe, husband?"

"They have gone," said Samuel sadly. "My completed work on the 'Life of Christ' is also lost. But at least we are all safe. We must thank God for that."

"My father's papers too — all I have left of him — have gone," Susanna croaked through smoke blackened lips. "We have nothing left now, husband, except our family."

Samuel rallied his thoughts. Briefly he had been overwhelmed with grief for his beloved books and all his work. But there were more important things. He knelt down and drew his family around him.

"Let us thank God for his great mercy in saving all our children. The house is nothing. We are rich enough."

"Come, Mama." Seventeen-year-old Emilia helped her mother up. "Can you walk?" she asked anxiously.

"With difficulty," Susanna gasped.

"We have a cart, mistress." One of the villagers came over and she and Emilia were helped aboard and the cart rumbled off to take Susanna to lodgings where she would stay for the next few months. She gazed sadly back at her scattered family and wondered when she would have them all around her again.

She slept fitfully on a strange mattress and woke late to find her husband bending over her.

"What shall we do?" asked Susanna in despair. "The family will have to be separated. None of the villagers can take all of us." Her voice was still reduced to a croak after all the smoke she had inhaled, but as usual her first care was for the family.

Samuel for once was practical. "Sukey and Hetty can go to London."

"To London?" queried Susanna, bewildered.

"My brother, Matthew, will, I am sure, welcome Hetty. He is very fond of her. Perhaps your brother, Samuel, will take Sukey. After all she bears your name and you were very close to him."

"I am sure he would but he plans to go to India soon. He works for the East India Company."

"Then when he leaves, Sukey can go to brother Matthew with Hetty. The villagers will take the younger children and you, my dear, will go into lodgings with Emilia. She is old enough to care for you when your time comes."

"I am afraid the children will learn disagreeable ways," sighed Susanna.

"We will hope not. I will rebuild a home for you as quickly as I can. The Church Commissioners will help. I have searched the ruins. A little lumber was saved below stairs; but not one rag above. The silver in your chest is moulded into a lump. I shall send it to Mr Hoare to sell for me."

"Is the barley safe?"

Samuel nodded. "Praise God. Above half of it is safe in the barns."

"Thank God. That will help a little."

"Mr Smith of Gainsborough has sent for some of the children."

"That is kind of him but it is sad that the family must be divided."

"It will be but for a short time," consoled Samuel. "Some of the neighbours have sent clothes for us. We are in the same state as Adam and Eve when they first set up house-keeping."

Susanna smiled. "At least the children are only a little burnt and will not be disfigured. And you were not hurt."

"I have only a small blister on my hand," admitted Samuel. He could not understand how he had escaped more serious injury.

Susanna touched the wound gently. "I am glad you were not hurt. What is that?" She indicated a blackened piece of paper he was holding.

"It is a sheet from my Polyglot Bible[23]. There is only one verse legible and it is in Latin. Listen. It says, 'Go sell all that thou hast; and take up thy cross and follow Me.' "

Tears pricked Susanna's eyes. "We do not need to sell, husband. We have lost nearly all we had. But the Lord has not deserted us. He is the rock on which we must build." She smiled through her tears. "He saved our children and plucked my precious son, John, as a brand from the burning."

"Amen," responded Samuel gruffly.

"Samuel, how did the fire start?"

His face darkened. "I met Mr Maw, the chief man of the town this morning. He accused me of firing the house myself."

"Oh Samuel. Why should he do that?"

"He said I had done it before to get money. It is a wicked lie, Sukey."

"Of course it is."

"I think it is either an accident or … " He hesitated.

"Yes?"

"I think perhaps Mr Maw thinks he knows who set fire to our house and he covers up his knowledge by accusing me."

Susanna shivered. "I wish they did not hate us so." She shut her eyes and Samuel looked sadly at her. He hoped the baby had not been damaged by her ordeal.

---

23   Bible with translations in several languages.

"I will leave you to sleep now, Sukey. Emilia, you will see to your mother."

"Yes Papa." Emilia watched her father leave the room. She loved him but like her mother, she did wish he was more practical. She wondered how long it would be before the Rectory was rebuilt. Meanwhile she and Susanna lived an easier life with the family who had offered them lodgings.

But Susanna was unhappy. She hated to accept charity. "We have nothing with which to pay our kind hosts or repay the tradesmen," she said sadly. "The twenty pounds I had taken such pains to save over many months was taken by the fire. What are we to do?"

"You must rest, mother. You will need your strength for the birth."

It was easy to say but difficult to do. Susanna lay and worried. Ever since her marriage she had been buffeted by difficulties and this last blow had proved almost too much for her. But with her indomitable courage she faced the bleak life ahead of her. In March, a few weeks after the fire, her last child was born.

"We shall name her Kezziah after one of the daughters of Job," announced Samuel as Susanna hugged the tiny scrap of humanity. She could not help thinking that her husband had something in common with the Old Testament patriarch. Things had not gone right for him either, had they?

A week later she attended her last service for the 'Churching of Women'. Little Kezziah, soon to be known as Kezzy, survived. She was not as intelligent as the others and Susanna wrote later that Kezzy 'was more *years* in learning than any of the rest had been *months*.'

It was not in Susanna's nature to remain idle; she had been shattered by the fire. but she had no intention of neglecting her spiritual health and one morning she wrote in her journal[24], 'Experience teaches you that it is absolutely necessary to spend a considerable time in spiritual exercises and therefore be careful to get and improve all opportunities of retirement and recollection.'

Her children continued to be her prime concern and she wrote, 'There is nothing I now desire to live for, but to do some small service to my children.' Five days after the catastrophe she wrote to Sammy at Westminster School, giving him an account of the fire but omitting details which he would have liked to have known. She was more interested in spending eight pages in inquiring after 'the health of (his) soul'.

She was also concerned that she was no longer able to teach her younger children so lengthy letters had to replace her daily instruction. Her sadness at having to do this shows in one of her letters to her fifteen year old daughter, Sukey. in London.

Dear Sukey,

Since our misfortunes have separated us from each other, and we can no longer enjoy the opportunities we once had of conversing together, I can no other way discharge the duty of a parent, or comply with my inclination of doing you all the good I can, but by writing.[25]

On ten closely written pages she gave an exposition of the Apostles' Creed, explaining in great detail what each item of belief meant. Her own spirituality and deep faith shone through the letter as did her concern for her daughter. She ended:

I cannot tell whether you have ever seriously considered the lost and miserable condition you are in by nature: if

---

24   Headingley Mss, Wesley College, Bristol
25   Jan 13th 1710, Headingley Mss, Wesley College, Bristol

you have not, it is high time to begin to do it; and I shall earnestly beseech the Almighty to enlighten your mind to renew and sanctify you by his Holy Spirit that you may be his child by adoption here, and an heir of his blessed kingdom hereafter.[26]

Sukey was instructed to send this letter to Sammy at Westminster School so he could copy it and imbibe its teaching. Her eldest son's spiritual welfare was very close to her heart. When she wrote to him again in October, she instructed him:

Begin and end the day with him who is the Alpha and Omega ... But above all things my dear Sammy, I command you, beg and beseech you to be very strict in your observance of the Lord's Day. I am verily persuaded that our most gracious God is more ready to grant our petitions ... on that Day.[27]

As well as writing to her children, Susanna spent time preparing a dissertation on the Ten Commandments which, she informed her daughter, Sukey, 'have been generally esteemed a summary of the Moral Law. Yet they are not all strictly speaking moral but the most of them are positive precepts founded on the moral law.'[28] Her dissertation formed the basis of a lengthy letter to Sukey.

Although Emilia was living in the same lodgings, she, too, did not escape instruction. She was able to converse with her mother but Susanna wrote down 'A Religious Conference between M. and E.' This was set out rather like a play with Emilia asking for instruction and her mother providing it.

---

26   ibid
27   ibid
28   Headingley Mss,Wesley College, Bristol

E: In obedience to your order, I come to be further in-
      structed in the principles of Religion … I hum-
      bly beg leave to require that things may be
      clearly and plainly provided before you de-
      mand my assent to the truth of them.

M: Provided you do not come to cavil or make objec-
      tions without or against reason, I am willing to
      allow what liberty you desire. But then I must
      tell you, that moral truths must be proved by
      moral arguments.[29]

The 'Conference', dealing with the laws and nature of God,
eventually covered sixty pages but before it was completed,
the new Rectory had been built and they were able to return
to their home.

---

29   ibid

CHAPTER SIX

Starting Again

Samuel had continued his parish duties after the fire and, as indomitable as his wife, he had already started to rewrite the work that had been lost. Nothing had remained of the structure or its contents so the house had been completely rebuilt. The Church Commissioners had contributed some money but most of it had been raised by benefactors including the Rector's previous patron, the Marquis of Normanby who was now the Duke of Buckingham. He apparently bore Samuel no ill-will for having been so discourteous to his mistress.

Susanna was still suffering from depression after the birth of her last child but she roused herself from her lethargy on the day she was to return to her home. As the carriage drove up to the rebuilt Rectory, she gazed at it in disbelief. It was built entirely of red brick and tiles had replaced the thatch on the roof.

"It is larger than our previous home, Samuel," she remarked thoughtfully. Unlike her husband, she had not seen any of the rebuilding.

"There are three staircases," said Samuel proudly. "And the garden contains apple and pear trees. There is also a surprise for you."

He handed her down from the carriage; she headed for the front door but he put his hand on her arm.

"Come, my dear. Let us walk in the garden for a while." He led her round the side of the house. "See Sukey, I have planted some mulberry trees for you. You remember that before you gave birth to our firstborn, you had a craving for them. I promised I would one day give you some and here they are."

"Oh Samuel, thank you." Tears stood in Susanna's eyes. She knew he had done this to help her overcome her depression and she was touched.

"Come and see the house." Like a boy he hurried off and she followed him.

They entered a large room and Susanna gazed around her and nodded. "We will need more furniture."

"I'm afraid the house will be sparsely furnished for some time," said her husband ruefully. "The building was very costly."

"We will manage," said his wife cheerfully. "Show me the rest of the house."

They went up to the second floor. Susanna was delighted that there were seven rooms so there would be plenty of room for her growing family.

"This will be my study." Samuel flung open the door and disclosed a room that already contained a desk and a chair but little else.

Susanna wandered across to the window and gazed out. "You can see the church from here — and one of the windmills," she remarked. She noticed a door beside the window and opened it to reveal a small cupboard. "Oh you even have pegs on which to hang your wigs. That is very useful."

"It will also serve to store my cloak and the books I hope to acquire."

"Where are we to sleep?" Susanna was not surprised that her husband's first priority was his study.

He led her out of the room and into another large room containing a bed and a chair. He indicated the beams in the ceiling.

"The wood came from houses which had been destroyed in Gainsborough. But see here, Sukey." She followed him out of the room and into another one. He pointed at the ceiling. "That beam came from part of a ship's keel. I think we should call it the 'Keel Room'."

"Whatever you like, dear. Show me the other rooms."

They went from room to room and then up another set of stairs to a large area with a stone floor. She shivered. "Brr. It is cold. But some of the children must sleep up here. Perhaps Hetty. The corn can also be stored where it will be kept cool and safe."

"There are four more rooms on this floor." He ushered her out and then led her down another staircase to the kitchen, where there was already a large oval table with chairs around it.

"This is large enough. What is this?" She opened another door and gazed at a large empty space. Her eyes brightened. "Samuel, this will be perfect for the school room."

"Certainly, my dear. I'm sure we shall soon be really comfortable here."

As all the furniture had been lost in the fire, the new house was very sparsely furnished as Susanna had noted. Thirteen years later she was to write to her brother, Samuel, that the house still had only half the furniture it needed. But at least the family was together again although Susanna's anxiety that the children would learn bad manners and poor ways of speaking proved to be true. They had become rough and uncouth and she was not impressed with the broad Lincolnshire accent they had acquired. She complained to her husband.

"Before that fatal dispersion of the children after the fire, we went on very well. Never were children in better order or in more subjection to their parents."

"They will be again, Sukey," soothed her husband.

"But while they were away, they were left at liberty to converse with servants and they learned to neglect a strict observance of the Sabbath. Worst of all, they were allowed to play with any children good or bad."

Samuel nodded. "You must introduce a strict regime. Their rude ways will not be reformed without some difficulty."

"I will need your help, Samuel."

"I am sorry my dear; I have to travel to London for Convocation."

"Oh not now, Samuel," cried Susanna in despair. "We need you here. Why must you go?"

But she knew it was useless to argue. He would go in spite of her appeals. She tightened her lips and set out to 'reform' her children alone. It was not an easy task but she was determined not to be beaten. The following day she gathered her family together and announced her new rules. "We shall all rise at five o'clock to read the Scriptures. Kezzy will stay with me and I will read to her. The older ones of you will take the younger and read with them a Psalm and a chapter from the Old or New Testaments. Each day I shall tell you which Psalm and which chapter to read. After that you will each retire to your rooms for your private prayers before we all join together for breakfast."

"Yes, Mama," the children murmured.

"Lessons will continue as usual from nine in the morning until noon and then again from two o'clock until five. You will all work hard to make up for the year you have lost."

"Yes, Mama."

It was uphill work and the children sometimes resented the lack of freedom they had enjoyed for the past year. To bring her erring family back to the straight and narrow path, Susanna introduced some 'bye-laws'. She read them out one evening after supper.

"Whoever is charged with a fault, of which they are guilty, if they confess it, and promise to amend, will not be beaten.

"No sinful action, as lying, pilfering at Church or disobedience and quarrelling etc. on the Lord's day shall ever pass unpunished.

"Every signal act of obedience shall always be commended and frequently rewarded, according to the merits of the case.

"If ever any child performs an act of obedience or does anything with an intention to please, though the performance was not well, yet the obedience and intention will be kindly accepted, and the child with sweetness directed how to do better for the future.

"Propriety must always be preserved; no one is suffered to invade the property of another in the smallest matter.

"Promises must be strictly observed." [30]

She looked round the table at the children. All had their eyes fixed upon her. She continued, "I believe that it is important for girls to have some education. Therefore none of the younger girls will be put to work in the house or garden until they can read. Then when they do have to work, they must apply the same diligence to that as to their reading."

---

30   Adam Clarke, *Memoirs of the Wesley Family*

The girls nodded. As they grew up, they would be able to do far more than read and, like their mother, most of them would enjoy stimulating discussions and be able to hold their own in private debate.

Susanna did not waste time. Lessons started straight away. She followed the same pattern of teaching as she had done formerly with one innovation. A Psalm was sung at the beginning and end of each day's schooling.

While she was trying to instil manners and knowledge into her young family, her husband, when he was there, was interfering with her methods. Never as patient as his wife, he would often lose his temper and roar at any argumentative child. As his wife was teaching her brood to think for themselves, this created problems — particularly with her star pupil, John, or Jacky as he was known. Even at a very young age, he would not accept anything unless he had carefully reasoned it out. This exasperated his father.

"You think to carry everything by dint of argument, boy," Samuel irritably told his son after a particularly acrimonious argument. Turning to his wife, he added sarcastically, "I protest, sweetheart, I think our Jack would not attend to the most pressing necessities of nature unless he could give a reason for it!"

He may have been right! One day Susanna offered her young son a pear from one of her trees. "Would you like that, Jacky?" she asked.

He looked solemnly at her. "I will think of it, Mama," he said thoughtfully.

She waited patiently, trying to hide a smile until at last the silent debate was over and he accepted the pear. Susanna's influence on this son was very great. In his later dealings with women, it is likely that none of them measured up to his enlightened mother.

For the seven winters following the fire, Samuel was in London while his family were, as his daughter Emilia wrote many years later, 'in intolerable want and affliction.' She obviously resented her father going to 'Convocations of blessed memory' and said that she 'learnt what it was to seek money for bread, seldom having any without such hardships in getting it that much abated the pleasure of it.'

She had little sympathy with her father's 'assuming to (himself) a dominion over (his) fellow creatures which never was designed by God'. Like her brother Jack to whom she was very close, she reasoned things out and came to the conclusion that 'my father will never be worth a groat, as the saying is, and we of the female part of the family be left to get our own bread or starve as we see fit.' [31]

One evening in 1710 before Samuel left on one of his frequent trips to London, he had an announcement to make to his wife.

"As I will be away for several months, I have arranged for a curate, Mr Inman, to deal with matters in the parish during my absence," he told her.

She nodded. The affairs of the parish were his concern; hers were her children and she soon had more problems. The following year there was an outbreak of smallpox in the village. Five of the children caught it and Susanna wore herself out nursing them. But she was as good a nurse as she was a teacher and they all recovered. She was relieved that none of them was left with the disfigurement that was the hallmark of the dreaded disease. When they recovered, she was determined they should not miss out on their spiritual education because their father was away. She made a deci-

---

31   Stevenson, *Memorials of the Wesley Family*

sion and one evening after supper, she explained it to her family.

"I have decided," she told them, "that on one evening each week I will speak with each of you on whatever are your own spiritual concerns. Kezzy is too young yet to understand but the rest of you will have an evening a week set aside for you individually. On Monday evening I will talk with Molly; on Tuesday with Hetty; Wednesday with Nancy; Thursday with Jacky; Friday with Patty; Saturday with Charles; and on Sunday I will speak with Emily and Sukey together."

She kept strictly to this schedule and these intimate evening talks left an indelible impression upon all her children. John, in particular, always remembered his Thursday evening sessions and often referred to them in later life. He remained very close to his mother and later, during his ministry, he frequently asked her advice. Many letters passed between them when John was in London and she was still in Epworth.

Her ministry to her children was of more value than that of the curate Samuel had installed in his place. Unlike the Rector he had replaced, Mr Inman had no deep conviction about the Christian faith. Having conducted a Sunday morning service, he considered his duty done for the week. His sermons were uninspiring and unvaried. His parishioners wearied of hearing yet again how important it was to pay one's debts and owe no one anything.

"How can he speak like that?" Emilia said crossly to her mother after one service. "It is so tactless when everyone knows Papa always owes money. I don't understand how Papa could have left him in charge."

"I do not think your father can have heard him preach," said Susanna tolerantly. "But I am not happy that he has abandoned the afternoon service."

"I think soon, no one will attend the morning service," mused Emilia. "The numbers go down each week."

"That is very true," sighed Susanna. "I think, dear, that we will meet together on Sunday afternoons to read the Bible and perhaps listen to one of the improving sermons your father has on his shelves."

Emilia frowned. "Just you and me, Mama?"

"Oh no, dear, all the children and, of course the servants."

Her daughter smiled. "I think that is an excellent idea. May I help you to choose some sermons?"

"Of course. We shall look now. We must choose the best and most awakening sermons we can find. Then I will prepare for a meeting this afternoon."

So later that afternoon, the children, Betty and Simon, the servant boy who helped in the house and grounds, were gathered around the kitchen table.

"Let us start by singing a psalm," announced Susanna. The voices filled the room and carried outside to the grounds.

Susanna then read some prayers from the Book of Common Prayer and they joined together in saying the Lord's Prayer. For their first service, Susanna had chosen one of Samuel's shorter sermons and afterwards she discussed it and the Bible passage to which it was related. The children also contributed to the discussion.

After the servants had left, Susanna remarked to her eldest daughter, "I believe the Lord was really with us this afternoon. He gave me the words to say."

The following day Simon asked to speak to Susanna. "If you please, ma'am," he said politely, "I told my parents about the meeting yesterday and they asked me to beg leave for them to attend next week."

Susanna looked startled. "Of course they may, Simon," she smiled.

The following Sunday Simon's parents were so impressed, they told their neighbours and as news of the meetings spread throughout the village more and more people attended until the little kitchen was crammed to bursting point.

"There must have been above two hundred people here today," Susanna remarked when their guests had finally departed.

"Many went away for lack of room," added Emilia

"I do not like to deny any who ask admittance but there is not room," Susanna agreed. She looked worried. "I do not wish to do anything without your father's knowledge and approval. I must write to acquaint him with our meetings and the circumstances out of which they arose."

She did so and Samuel's reply was mixed. While commending her zeal, he considered the Sunday meetings would look 'particular' because she was a woman taking a man's role. He suggested that perhaps she could find a man to read the sermons. As he held a public position and was currently at Convocation, Samuel was afraid his wife's new role might damage his position.

Susanna demolished his arguments. Sitting down at her table, she wrote,

As to its looking *particular,* I grant it does; and so does almost everything that is serious, or that may any way advance the glory of God, or the salvation of souls, if it be performed out of a pulpit, or in the way of common conversation; because in our corrupt age the utmost care and diligence have been used to banish all discourse of God or spiritual concerns out of society, as if religion were never to appear out of the closet, and we were to be ashamed of nothing so much as of professing ourselves to be Christians.

To his objection that she was a woman, she reminded him,

I am also mistress of a large family. And though the superior charge of the souls contained in it lies upon you as head of the family, and as their minister, yet in your absence I cannot but look upon every soul you leave under my care, as a talent committed to me under a trust by the great Lord of all the families of heaven and earth. And if I am unfaithful to Him, or to you, in neglecting to improve these talents, how shall I answer unto Him, when He shall command me to render an account of my stewardship?

After a short pause during which she prayed earnestly that she might be given the right words to write to her erratic husband, she continued,

I thought it my duty to spend some part of the day in reading to and instructing my family, especially in your absence, when having no afternoon's service, we have so much leisure for such exercises; and such time I esteemed spent in a way more acceptable to God than if I had retired to my own private devotions.

This was the beginning of my present practice; other people coming and joining with us was purely accidental. Our lad told his parents — they first desired to be admitted; then others who heard of it, begged leave also; so our company increased to about thirty, and seldom exceeded forty last winter. But it has increased greatly since.

With those few neighbours who then came to me I discoursed more freely and affectionately than before. I chose the best and most awakening sermons we had, and I spent more time with them in such exercises. Since this our company has increased every night; for I dare deny none that asks admittance. Last Sunday, I believe we had above two hundred and yet many went away for want of room.

We meet not on any worldly design; we keep close to the business of the day; and as soon as it is over, they all go home. Where is the harm in this?

She picked up her husband's letter again and shook her head over his proposal to 'let some other person read'. "He does not consider what a people these are," she reflected. She would have to be straight with him.

Suppressing a smile, she wrote,

I do not think one man among them could read a sermon, without *spelling* a good part of it; and how would that edify the rest? Nor has any of our family a voice strong enough to be heard by such a number of people.

There was, however, one aspect of her ministry about which she was not happy. Because of her sex, she was not sure it was 'proper' for her 'to present the prayers of the people to God'. She concluded her letter by referring to this.

Last Sunday, I fain would have dismissed them before Prayers; but they begged so earnestly to stay, that I durst not deny them.[32]

Samuel's reply came more quickly than she expected but it was more in response to a strongly worded letter from his curate than a thoughtful comment on her own letter. Mr Inman was furious at the usurping of his position and wrote that the Rector's wife was 'turning the parsonage into a conventicle' and 'causing scandal in the parish and neighbourhood'.

Ignoring Susanna's carefully reasoned justification of her meetings, Samuel took fright and ordered his wife to stop the services. When Susanna read his letter, her lips tightened. She had no intention of being browbeaten and

32   Adam Clarke, *Memoirs of the Wesley Family*

was convinced that what she was doing was God's will. She had no doubt who was behind Samuel's change of heart.

It was about ten days before she deigned to reply and her annoyance was clear. Her quill flew angrily over the paper.

> I shall not enquire how it was possible that you should be prevailed on by the senseless clamours of two or three of the worst of your Parish to condemn what you so lately approved … I do not hear of more than three or four persons who are against our Meeting, of whom *Inman* is the chief. He … may call it a Conventicle; but we hear no outcry here, nor has any one said a word against it to me. And what does their calling it a Conventicle signify? Does it alter the nature of the thing? Or do you think that what *they* say is a sufficient reason to forbear a thing that has already done much good, and by the blessing of God may do much more?

Her language became even stronger. Her husband was miles away in London and had no idea of the true situation in Epworth. He must be told.

> It is plain … that this one thing has brought more people to Church, than ever anything did, in so short a time. We used not to have above twenty or twenty-five at evening service, whereas we have now between two and three hundred; which are more than ever came before to hear *Inman* in the morning.

Putting her quill down, she stared dreamily ahead of her, reflecting on the change the Meetings had on the villagers' attitude to the Wesleys. Her husband should know of it. How dare he criticise something that was doing so much good. She wrote:

> Our Meeting has wonderfully conciliated the minds of this people towards us, so that we now live in the greatest amity imaginable; and what is still better, they are very much reformed in their behaviour on the Lord's Day; and those who used to be playing in the streets now come to

hear a good sermon read, which is surely more acceptable to Almighty God ...

Some families who seldom went to Church, now go
constantly; and one person who had not been there for
seven years, is now prevailed upon to go with the rest.[33]

Clasping her hands together, she bowed her head. "Oh
Lord," she whispered. "Give me the right words to say for
if we stop the Meetings it may do great harm." In fairness
to her husband, she felt she had to make the points he had
obviously missed.

I need not tell you the consequences, if you determine to
put an end to our Meetings. You may easily perceive what
prejudice it may raise in the minds of these people
against Inman especially, who has had so little wit as to
speak publicly against it. I can now keep them to the
Church; but if it be laid aside, I doubt they will ever go to
hear him more, at least those who come from the lower
end of the Town.

She ended with a strongly worded appeal to her husband.
He would find it hard to resist.

If you do, after all, think fit to dissolve this assembly, do
not tell me that you *desire me* to do it for that will satisfy
my conscience. But send me your *positive command,* in
such full and express terms, as may absolve me from all
guilt and punishment, for neglecting this opportunity of
doing good, when you and I shall appear before the great
and awful tribunal of our Lord Jesus Christ.[34]

Laying down her pen, she commended her letter to God and
prayed that Samuel would not 'command' her to discontinue

---

33   Adam Clarke, *Memoirs of the Wesley Family*

34   Adam Clarke, *Memoirs of the Wesley Family*

the Meetings. How could he do so in view of her uncompromising words at the end of her letter?

She heard no more from him and the Meetings continued until he returned when Susanna was quite happy to relinquish the parish again into the Rector's care. The Meetings were replaced by evening services at the Church and Samuel found himself preaching to a larger congregation than ever before and the attitude of the villagers had changed.

"They are no longer hostile to us, Sukey," he said after the first evening service.

"They care for us now," she agreed. "I am so glad our little Meetings were of some help."

The Reverend Inman was still in the village and the parishioners, now that the Rector had returned, were determined he should understand their complaints about the curate.

"He preaches nothing except the duty of paying our debts and behaving well to our neighbours," they complained. "We think, Sir, there is more to religion than this."

"There certainly is," Samuel agreed. "I will hear him preach next Lord's Day and I myself will give him the text on which I wish him to preach".

The text he chose was from the Epistle to the Hebrews chapter eleven and verse six. *Without faith it is impossible to please him (God).*

The following Lord's Day Susanna sat in the front pew waiting for the sermon. She was not surprised to hear the curate announce in sonorous tones. "Faith, friends, is a most excellent virtue and it produces other virtues also. In particular it makes a man pay his debts."[35]

---

35   *The Life and Times of Samuel Wesley* by Luke Tyerman

That was the last sermon the Reverend Inman preached at Epworth!

CHAPTER SEVEN

The Rectory Ghost

Two years later in 1714, it was John's turn to fly the nest and once again Samuel's patron, the Duke of Buckingham came to the rescue. He was one of the governors of Charterhouse School in London and it was his turn to nominate likely candidates for the school and he considered Samuel Wesley's second son a suitable applicant. John was nearly eleven and he had been well taught by his mother since he was five in all but the classics. His father had taken care of his education in Latin and Greek. He was accepted and was enrolled at the school. Susanna was relieved that his education would not add to their debts as the Duke of Buckingham would take care of all the fees.

Like all public schools of the day, Charterhouse had a tough regime. However the rigorous education which followed his mother's sound teaching served as an excellent training for the boy who was to become such a renowned preacher.

Sammy had now returned to Westminster School as a teacher — or usher — as it was called in that place. He was a generous man and from his first salary he sent home money to help with the Epworth finances. He continued to prop up his family financially for the rest of his life.

Soon after he started at Westminster he met a neighbour, the Reverend John Berry and was introduced to his daughter, Ursula. They fell in love and were married in 1715. It was a very happy marriage. Susanna was delighted when she heard the news but sad that she was unable to attend the wedding of her firstborn. Even after his marriage Sammy continued to send money to his parents and his wife apparently made no objection.

Susanna missed her sons but life at the Rectory went on as normal and Susanna continued to teach and to counsel her family. A new man servant, Robin, and a new maid, Nanny Marshall, were engaged in November 1716. The other servant, Betty Massy was still with them.

On 1st December Molly and her older sister, Sukey, who had been named after their mother, were sitting in the dining room when Nanny Marshall, holding a bowl of butter rushed into the room in a very distraught state.

"O Miss," she gasped. "I'm so frightened. It sounds as though there's someone dying in the 'all."

Molly looked up from her embroidery. "How can someone be dying out there?"

"But it *sounds* like it, Miss. It's an awful groaning sound and there's someone knocking at the door. I 'eard it, I tell you."

"All right, Nanny. Calm yourself." Sukey took charge. "I'm sure there's nothing there."

She led them out of the room and they stood and listened. The only sound was that of the wind howling outside.

"I expect it was the wind you heard," said Molly kindly.

The girl sniffed. "I s'pose so, Miss, but it sounded ever so real."

She returned to the kitchen and the girls returned to their work thinking no more of the disturbance.

The following day Nanny Marshall was sitting with Robin in the kitchen when they both heard a knocking at the door and some groaning.

"It is Mr Turpine," comforted Robin. "He often groans so when he uses the stone for the knife sharpening."

"But he wouldn't come now." Nanny's eyes were wide and frightened.

Robin opened the door but there was no one there and the noise continued. Eventually it stopped and they went to bed. Robin went last and as he reached the top of the garret stairs, he blinked. A few feet away he could see a handmill whirling merrily round. Shaking his head, he continued to bed but was disturbed by noises.

"It sounded like the gobbling of a turkey cock," he told the two maids the next day. "Then it seemed as if someone was stumbling over my boots and shoes but I'd left them downstairs."

"Did you see anything in your room?" asked Nanny Marshall, her eyes wide with fright.

Robin shook his head. "There was no one there."

"It's like last night when we heard the knocking. I'm frightened."

Betty Massey, the other maid, laughed heartily as she looked sceptically at them. "What a couple of fools you are," she scoffed. "I defy anything to frighten *me*."

But her turn was to come. That evening after she had finished churning, she put the butter in the tray. No sooner had she carried it into the dairy than she heard a knocking above and below the shelf where the casks of milk stood. Taking her candle she searched around the shelf but could find nothing. Hurriedly dropping the butter tray which she was still holding, she rushed back to the kitchen where Nanny Marshall gazed at her in amazement.

"Whatever's the matter?" she asked.

"I heard it too — the knocking — on the milk shelf but there was nothing there."

The disturbances continued and were heard by other members of the household. A few days later as Molly and Sukey were in the bedroom they shared, Sukey suddenly said, "Will you promise not to laugh if I tell you something?"

Molly looked up from the book she was reading. "Of course. What is it?"

"Yesterday when Nancy and I were in the dining room, we heard a noise at the door. It sounded like something rushing past the doors that open into the garden. Then there were three loud knocks, immediately followed by another three and in half a minute, the same number over our heads. We went out to see if anybody had been in the garden or in the room above us but nobody had been there."

"I wonder you are so easily frighted," said Molly scornfully. "I would fain see what would fright me."

She had hardly spoken when both girls were startled by three bouncing thumps under their feet.

Sukey flew across the room and jumped into bed without removing her clothes. Molly hastily followed. Sukey's teeth were chattering for fear. "Th — that's what I heard downstairs. Oh look." She pointed at the warming pan beside the bed which was performing a little dance by itself.

"And the latch on the door is going up and down," gasped Molly.

Sukey buried her head under the bedclothes as the whole house rattled and shook.

After a while the noise died down and the only sound was that of the wind; the girls slept fitfully that night.

A few days later Molly was reading by herself in the dining room when she heard the door open and shut. Looking towards it, she realised it was still closed and no one had entered. The hair stood up on her neck as around her she heard another softer noise. It was as if someone was walking round her with a silk night-gown trailing upon the ground; but she could see nothing.

Gritting her teeth, she thought to herself, "It signifies nothing to run away; for whatever it is, it can run faster than I can."

Slowly she rose, put her book under her arm and walked calmly away. After supper, she told Sukey what had happened.

"You didn't see anything?" her sister queried.

"No, there was nothing there."

"Let's go to bed. Perhaps we can sleep before it starts knocking again."

Hetty was the next to be plagued by their unwanted visitor. The following night she waited, as was her custom, outside her father's study on the second floor to take away his candle. It was about half past nine and suddenly she heard footsteps coming down the garret steps. At each step the house shook from top to bottom. The steps passed her and went down the front stairs; then she heard them go up the back stairs. As they passed her on the garret stairs, she thought she could see a man wearing a white night-gown trailing after him but he disappeared out of her sight and the steps faded.

Her legs felt as if they were pinned to the ground and she gasped as she suddenly heard her father's knock. It was the signal for her to receive his candle. Trembling, she rose to her feet and entered his study but she was afraid to say anything about what had happened. She hastily took the candle and went to bed as quickly as possible.

The next day she told her eldest sister Emilia what had happened. Emilia shook her head. "You know, I believe none of these things. Pray let me take away the candle tonight and I will find out the trick."

So that night it was Emilia who waited outside her father's study. No sooner had she collected his candle than she heard a noise below her. She hastened down the stairs to the hall where the noise appeared to be. When she reached it, the noise was in the kitchen. Always it seemed to elude her.

Then she heard a knocking at the back door. She opened it but there was no one there. Trying to shut it, she felt as though someone was pushing it open. Breathing heavily, she set her knee and shoulder against it forcing it shut. Then she turned the key. Immediately the knocking started again. She stared at the door for several minutes as the knocking continued. Then, shrugging her shoulders, she turned her back on it and went up to bed, convinced that her sisters and the servants had not imagined the noises they said they had heard.

Their mother had to be told, she decided. So about ten days after Nanny Marshall had first heard the groaning and knocking, Susanna was told of the events in her home. She was sitting in her room when Emilia knocked at the door.

Bidden to enter, she did not waste time. "Mama, the servants and the children have been several times frightened with strange groans and knockings about the house."

Susanna looked calmly at her eldest daughter. "If I hear anything myself, I shall know how to judge," she said.

"But Mama, last night I heard the knocking too and when I opened the back door, I could not easily shut it again. It was as if someone was thrusting it back against me."

"The wind is very strong up here, dear. As for the other noises, they are no doubt made by the rats that John Maw has frightened out of his house nearby. They must have come into ours. He used a horn to frighten them so I will order that one be sent for."

"Very well, Mama."

The horn was acquired but Molly was very displeased about it. "If the thing is supernatural, it certainly will be very angry and more troublesome."

Susanna ignored the warning and ordered the instrument to be blown in the garrets where the rats were most likely to be. The noise was tremendous but unfortunately it had no effect. Molly was right. The day after the horn had been blown Emilia went to her mother at seven o'clock in the morning.

"Mama, Molly was right. Whereas before, the noises were always in the night now they are in the day time as well. Please come to the nursery where you will hear for yourself that we are not startled at nothing."

Susanna followed her daughter to the nursery and now she too heard a knocking — first at the foot of the bed and then immediately at its head.

"If you are a spirit, answer me," she commanded. She stamped her foot on the ground several times and when she stopped, the knocking copied the pattern of her stamping exactly. She repeated the stamping and the same thing happened.

Kezzy, now six, who was sitting on her bed now jumped off and cried, "Let it answer me too, if it can."

She stamped her little foot and once again the sounds were repeated in exact detail. Kezzy laughed and did it again. She thought it was a fascinating game.

"That's enough, Kezzy," snapped Susanna. She looked under the bed and the hair on the back of her neck pricked as she saw something like a headless badger run out from under the bed and hide under Emilia's petticoats. She glanced quickly at her daughters but none of them appeared to have seen anything.

"The other night, Mama," said Sukey who had been standing by the window, "I heard a knocking just under my feet. I knew the room below was locked so I was frightened and leapt into bed with all my clothes on. Then it sounded as if a great chain had fallen. Last night I resolved to lie here in the nursery. Late at night I heard several strong knocks on the two lowest steps of the garret stairs outside the nursery. Then there was a knocking within the room and it came gradually to sister Hetty's bed and she trembled strongly in her sleep."

Susanna listened thoughtfully to her daughter. What was happening? Did the sounds portend evil to someone? Was her husband in danger? Had something happened to her sons? She shut her eyes and said a quick prayer. If anyone was in danger, she reflected, it was more likely to be her brother, Samuel, who had gone to India with the East India Company. She had not heard from him for some time.

Opening her eyes, she smiled at her daughters.

"I believe we have a spirit of some kind but what to do I am not yet sure. I will decide whether to tell your father."

She left the room anxiously debating if she should let Samuel know what had been happening in his house. The reason she hesitated was because she knew that if it boded any ill to him, he would not be able to bear it. She did not want to inform him of it lest he should fancy it was against his own death—which indeed she feared.

After their mother had left, Emilia said suddenly, "I think perhaps it is old Jeffrey who is plaguing us."

"Old Jeffrey?" queried Sukey.

"He worked in the garden. You remember? He died not long ago. I shall call our visitor 'Old Jeffrey'."

"I like Old Jeffrey," announced Kezzy. "He plays games with me."

The others looked at her. They did not share her views. However, later in the day when Sukey heard a knocking, she ran to find her youngest sister and said, "Hark Kezzy, Jeffrey is knocking above."

Kezzy immediately ran up the stairs and then down again. Wherever she went, the knocking was always a little ahead of her. "There is no better diversion than this," she declared as the knocking finally stopped and she sat down, breathless.

Over the next few days the spirit — or whatever it was — continued to knock and groan frequently at all hours of the day and night. Samuel had still not heard it and Susanna was determined that her meditations should not be disrupted. She prayed earnestly that she would not be disturbed between five and six in the evening and, to her relief, there was never any noise in her chamber during that time while she was at her devotions. But she decided her husband should be told.

Choosing a time when they were together in their bedroom preparing for bed, Susanna did not waste words. "I have decided you should be told of this, Samuel. For several days now there have been strange noises in the house. The children only told me of them recently. The servants have heard groaning and footsteps up and down the stairs. There is knocking in the nursery and downstairs Emilia had the door thrust back against her when she tried to shut it. I thought it was rats and had a horn blown in the garret but the disturbances have worsened. It is right that you should know."

Samuel's response was predictable. "Sukey, I am ashamed of you," he said angrily. "These boys and girls frighten one another but you are a woman of sense. Let me hear of it no more."

Until this time he had been the only member of the family who had not been disturbed. His turn was to come. The next night family prayers were said as usual at six o'clock. As Samuel began the prayer for the King, a knocking began all round the room. Angrily, Samuel glared at his family to see who had interrupted the prayers. All were still. He began again with the same result. In the end he was shouting to drown out the thunderous banging that accompanied the 'Amen'. As he finished, he glared at his wife. He hadn't forgotten she had once refused to say 'Amen' to the prayer for the King. Obviously their visitor did not share her views.

Now that the Rector had been introduced to their un-wanted guest, it wouldn't leave him alone. That night he and Susanna had just gone to bed when they were startled by a series of knocks. It sounded as if someone had struck violently on a wooden chest with a large stick.

Samuel leapt up. "What was that? It sounds as though someone is in the house but all the family have been in bed for several hours. Come Susanna."

He did not wait for a reply but lit a candle and carrying a stout stick, he left the room with Susanna following him. The knocking continued. It seemed that as they went into one chamber, the knocking came from the one they had just left.

As they were going downstairs, Susanna stopped and gasped.

"What is it?" whispered Samuel.

"It felt as though someone has just emptied a bag of coins at my feet."

Samuel lowered the candle. "There is nothing there."

"No."

As they reached the bottom of the stairs, there was a tremendous crash as if all the bottles under the stairs had been dashed into a thousand pieces. But all were still whole.

At the bottom of the stairs their mastiff came to meet them whimpering and trying to hide behind Susanna. With the dog trailing them, they went into all the rooms on the ground floor and then upstairs into all the children's rooms. They were all asleep.

Susanna bent over Kezzy. "See how she pants and trembles in her sleep."

"I think they all do," said Samuel solemnly.

Returning to their room, Samuel set the candle on the table and looked at his wife. His face was pale.

"I will ask the Reverend Joseph Hoole from Haxey to stay one night with me. I will not have my house terrified by an unseen presence."

The next day was Christmas Day and in the evening Samuel decided on an experiment. At prayers he omitted the prayers for the King and was allowed to speak uninterrupted. But 'Old Jeffrey' as Emilia insisted on calling him, had not finished with him yet. As he sat at supper, the plate in front of him suddenly started to dance upon the table. All stared in amazement but Betty, the maid, who was clearing the places, took it away as it came to rest and spoilt the fun. Kezzy giggled and Susanna looked reprovingly at her.

The next evening as Samuel sat in his study, he heard the knocking in the next room. Going in, he found fourteen year old Nancy alone. She looked pale but calm in the flickering of the candle light. By now the girls were used to the knocking which usually started between nine and ten at night. It became so familiar that they would say, "Jeffrey is coming; it is time to sleep."

Samuel looked at his daughter. "Let us see if it will speak, Nancy," he said. In a loud voice, he commanded, "Speak, spirit, if you hear."

There was no sound. Moving towards his daughter, he said to her, "These spirits love darkness; put out the candle and perhaps it will speak."

"Yes, Papa."

When she had done so, Samuel repeated his command but still there was silence. He thought for a moment and then said, "Nancy, two Christians are an overmatch for the devil. Go downstairs. it may be when I am alone, he will have courage to speak."

When she had gone, he remembered Susanna's fears. Dare he test the spirit? His heart pounding, he made his decision. "If thou art the spirit of my son, Samuel, I pray knock three knocks and no more."

Hardly daring to breathe, he waited. No knocking was heard. He gave a sigh of relief but he was not really happy about what he had done. Had not the Lord been very angry with Saul when he had called up the spirit of the dead Samuel? A Christian should have no dealings with the spirits of the dead. He knew that and resolved not to be tempted again.

The following evening it was Robin's turn again. As he sat alone by the fire in the kitchen, he was startled by a movement. Something like a small rabbit with ears laid flat upon its neck scuttled out of the copper, the metal boiler where Betty did the laundry. As Robin watched, bemused, it turned swiftly round five times. Galvanised into action at last, the man servant leapt up and grabbed the tongs to catch it but it had disappeared. Shaking with fear, he went to find Betty to tell her about the latest manifestation. She was sewing in the parlour.

"Do you think I should tell the master?" he asked. "He now knows about the spirit."

Betty shook her head. "I think he knows enough."

"He has told me to go to Mr Hoole, the vicar of Haxey, to say that Mr Wesley desires his company tomorrow evening. Perhaps *he* will be able to help."

"He is a very pious and sensible man," said Betty thoughtfully.

The next night Mr Hoole appeared. It was 28th December 1716. The younger children went to bed at their usual time but the rest of the family sat in the parlour regaling their visitor with the events of the past few days.

Just before ten o'clock Robin came in and said, "Old Jeffrey is coming for I hear the signal."

Mr Hoole looked puzzled.

"Jeffrey was an old man who worked here and died," explained Susanna. "Emily decided that he might be plaguing us so that is why she gave him that name and now the children and the servants always use it."

A gentle knocking was now heard above their heads.

"Is that *it*?" their visitor enquired in a hushed tone.

"Yes," replied Susanna. She listened to the sounds. "But it is much lower than usual."

"But it can still be heard clearly even when we are talking."

Samuel caught up a candle and stood up. "Come, Sir, now you shall hear properly for yourself."

He led the apprehensive Mr Hoole upstairs leaving Susanna and her elder daughters downstairs. Entering the nursery where Hetty, Nancy and Patty slept, they heard the knocking clearly at the head of the bed. Although the girls were asleep, they were trembling and Samuel became very angry.

Pulling out a pistol, he aimed it at the place from where the sound came but Mr Hoole caught his arm in horror. "Sir, you are convinced this is something supernatural. If so, you cannot hurt it; but you give it power to hurt you."

Samuel was still angry but he accepted the truth of what had been said. Putting the pistol away, he went close to the bed head saying in a low, stern voice, "Thou deaf and dumb devil, why dost thou fright these children that cannot answer for themselves? Come to me in my study that am a man."

He led Mr Hoole into his study and immediately there were a series of knocks identical to the knock he always gave to let his wife know he had arrived home. Samuel looked triumphantly at his visitor. "You hear for yourself. What am I to do?"

Mr Hoole did not reply immediately. Then he said, "Mr Wesley, I think you should leave this house."

"No!" exclaimed Samuel. "Let the devil flee from me. I will never flee from the devil."

Why neither he nor the vicar from Haxey did not call on the name of the Lord Jesus Christ to cast out the evil spirit is a mystery; there is no evidence that at any time a serious attempt was made to exorcise this irritating poltergeist. As Samuel showed his guest where he was to sleep, he wondered if the sounds portended evil. Susanna was sure that one of her sons or her brother had met with some mishap.

Whether Samuel's attempts at communication had worked or whether the fact that he refused to move had influenced it, the sounds were heard no more after that day. There seemed no rational explanation for either their starting or finishing. The family was able to return to normal but Susanna was still concerned that some harm might have come to one of her family.

But on January 12th 1717 a letter arrived. It was to Susanna from her eldest son. Greatly relieved to hear that he was well, she promptly retired to her chamber to write to him.

Dear Sam,

This evening we were agreeably surprised with your packet which brought the welcome news of your being alive, after we had been in the greatest panic imaginable, almost a month, thinking either you were dead or one of your brothers by some misfortune been killed.

She continued to give the reason for her fears followed by a detailed account of 'Old Jeffrey's' visit. She concluded:

'Thus it continued till the 28th December, when it loudly knocked (as your father used to do at the gate) in the nursery, and departed. We have various conjectures what this may mean. For my own part, I fear nothing now you are safe at London hitherto, and I hope God will still preserve you. Though sometimes I am inclined to think my brother is dead. Let me know your thoughts on it.

Sammy had no explanation but was fascinated by the phenomenon and wrote to his mother again demanding to know more; in a postscript he added, 'Have you dug in the place where the money seemed poured at your feet?' Susanna very properly ignored this worldly suggestion!

He wrote to his father:

Dear Sir,

My mother tells me a very strange story of disturbances in your house. I wish I could have some more particulars from you. I would thank Mr Hoole if he would favour me with a letter concerning it. Not that I want to be confirmed myself in the belief of it, but for any other person's satisfaction. My mother sends to me to know my thoughts of it, and I cannot think at all of any interpretation. Wit, I fancy, may find many, but wisdom, none.

Your dutiful and loving son,

S. Wesley

That the Rector had been disturbed by the affair was clear from his reply to his son. He did not reply as promptly as his wife and unlike hers, his letter was not detailed but he was concerned enough to keep a detailed journal of the occurrences. He wrote briefly to Sammy:

> Dear Sam,
>
> As for the noises in our family, I thank God we are now all quiet. There were some surprising circumstances in that affair. Your mother has not written you a third part of it. When I see you here, you shall see the whole account, which I wrote down. It would make a glorious penny book for Jack Dunton! But while I live, I am not ambitious for anything of that nature. I think that's all, but blessings from
>
> Your loving Father,
>
> Sam. Wesley

Sammy was too impatient to wait to hear what his father had to say and wrote to all his sisters requesting information 'about the spirit'. 'I cannot think any of you very superstitious,' he wrote, 'unless you are much changed since I saw you.'

His sisters were only too happy to oblige and wrote him detailed accounts of their own experiences. Emilia, particularly, was relieved at being able to set down her thoughts about what had happened. She wrote:

> I am so far from being superstitious that I was too much inclined to infidelity, so that I heartily rejoice at having such an opportunity of convincing myself, past doubt or scruple, of the existence of some beings besides those we see. A whole month was sufficient to convince anybody of the reality of the thing; and to try all ways of discovering any trick, had it been possible for any such to have been used. I shall only tell you what I myself heard and leave the rest to others.

Having detailed the behaviour of the 'spirit', she continued,

If you would know my opinion of the reason for this, I shall briefly tell you. I believe it to be witchcraft, for these reasons. About a year since, there was a disturbance at a town near us, that was undoubtedly witches; and if so near, why may they not reach us? Then my father had for several Sundays before its coming preached warmly against consulting those that are called cunning men, which our people are given to; and it had a particular spite at my father.

Samuel was determined to find a rational explanation for the events. 'Was there never a new maid or man in the house that might play tricks?' he asked his mother. Susanna discounted this.

We had both man and maid new this last Martinmas (St Martin's Day, 11th November) yet I do not believe either of them occasioned the disturbance ... because they were more affrighted than anybody else. Besides, we have often heard the noises when they were in the room by us; and the maid particularly was in such a panic that she was almost incapable of all business, nor durst ever go from one room to another, or stay by herself a minute after it began to be dark.

She also felt 'it was beyond the power of any human creature to make such strange and various noises.' Susanna eventually wearied of her son's persistent questions and on 27th March she wrote to him,

I cannot imagine how you should be so curious about our unwelcome guest. For my part, I am quite tired with hearing or speaking of it; but if you come among us, you will find enough to satisfy all your scruples, and perhaps may hear or see it yourself.

She was still convinced that the noises and disturbances portended the death of her brother and in view of later events, she was convinced she was right. Christian though she undoubtedly was, she was still influenced by the superstitious atmosphere of the eighteenth century when witches were still hunted and burnt and any unusual happenings were always regarded as supernatural and their meanings sought.

The explanation for the Epworth poltergeist has never been found. At one time the family had thought perhaps the villagers were playing a trick on them or even the new servants, Robin and Nanny, were instrumental in the knocking. However the servants' fear seemed real so, as Susanna told Sammy, they had to be discounted.

The experience seems to have affected Emilia more than any of the rest of the family and years later in another letter to her brother she referred to 'that wonderful thing, called by us 'Jeffrey'' saying, 'So little is known of the invisible world that I at least am not able to judge whether it be a friendly or an evil spirit.'

Whatever it was, it eventually stopped its tormenting of the Wesley family and none of their neighbours ever heard it.[36]

---

36   The above account of 'Old Jeffrey' has been adapted from
      Adam Clarke's *Memoirs of the Wesley Family*

CHAPTER EIGHT

Whatever Happened to Susanna's Brother?

Soon after the ghost episode Sukey left home to pay a visit to her Uncle Matthew with whom she had stayed after the disastrous fire of 1709. She had not then stayed long with Samuel Annesley as he had gone to India soon after the fire. In London she enjoyed the luxurious living that her uncle, who was now a widower, could provide for her; the comforts that could be found in his house in Johnson's Court were sadly lacking at Epworth. She also looked forward to the day when her Uncle Samuel Annesley would return from India and provide handsomely for her as he had promised. Unfortunately she was to be disappointed.

Samuel Wesley's stewardship of his brother-in-law's business affairs had proved as disastrous as Susanna had predicted. She had warned her brother that Samuel was no businessman and that he lived too far from London to be able to deal adequately with Annesley's affairs. This proved to be the case and Annesley was so enraged by the misman-agement of his affairs that he dismissed Samuel and engaged another agent. He also declared he would now have to consider whether or not he would assist his nieces and sisters financially in the future.

Samuel, annoyed at the accusations hurled at him, threw the letter at Susanna who read it with increasing dismay.

"Oh Samuel, I warned you not to become his agent. Now we have no prospects. What is to become of us?"

Increasingly worn out with the frustration of trying to care for her family with such limited means and with little help from her husband, Susanna was near tears. She had not felt well for some time and this was the last straw.

Samuel, who also was becoming frailer, did not reply, but stared glumly out of the window. He knew that the prospect of eventual financial help from her brother had been something for his wife to anticipate with eagerness. Now it looked as though even that slim hope had been snatched from her.

Susanna looked at the letter again. "These things are unkind, very unkind. How cruel of him to say you are 'apt to rest upon deceitful promises' and 'are not fit for worldly business'. I shall write to tell him of my displeasure even though the unhappy differences between you both have prevented my writing for some years."

Samuel sighed, his anger gone. "He is right though, Sukey. I should not have taken on the task of being his agent. But I was never knowingly deceitful."

"I know you were not, dear, and so I shall tell him."

"The girls must know that there is now little hope of help from their uncle."

Susanna nodded. "I shall tell them and I will write to Sukey and Emilia."

When Sukey received her mother's letter, she was horrified; bursting into tears, she rushed upstairs and threw herself on her bed. What was she to do now? Sitting up, she dried her eyes and stared out of the window. She was now in her mid twenties and she did not want to die an old maid. She would have to marry well but she had little chance of a good match now that she had no dowry from her Uncle Samuel to bring to her husband. She was sure she could now expect nothing from him in spite of his earlier promises.

Since she had come to London, she had been courted by several young men, but the one who had the best prospects to offer a wife was Richard Ellison. He was a gentleman from a good family; he farmed his own estate and had a very respectable establishment. Sukey considered his estates brought in enough money to keep her in the style to which she had become accustomed.

He had already proposed to her but she had not given him a definite answer. Preoccupied with material comfort, she shut her eyes to the fact that although good looking, he was uncouth and coarse in his manner. She was sure that when they were married, she could reform him.

That night when he came to supper at her uncle's house, he again proposed to her and to his amazement she accepted him.

"We'll be married straight away!" he exclaimed, delighted. "There's no point in waiting. Do you hear that, everyone? Sukey is to marry me. I shall get a special licence tomorrow."

Her uncle disapproved strongly but was powerless to prevent Sukey's rash marriage.

"I fear you will not be happy, Sukey," he said bluntly. "I wish you had never met him."

But nothing would dissuade Sukey; she and Richard Ellison were married in 1719. After their marriage the couple went to Epworth where they were received politely by her parents. Susanna and Samuel were horrified that their beautiful daughter had cast herself away on a man who treated his wife no better than one of his farm animals. He was rude and overbearing and Sukey soon knew she had made a bad mistake but there was nothing she could do. She was tied to him for life. Divorce at that time was practically unknown and married women had no rights. The husband dominated every aspect of their lives.

In 1720 John finished his schooling at Charterhouse and entered Oxford on a Charterhouse scholarship. Soon afterwards Emilia, too, left Epworth for London to stay with her Uncle Matthew. She hoped to find a post as a governess. While there she met Robert Leybourne who was a friend of her brother, John. She fell deeply in love with him and her love was reciprocated. She could not find work in London so she returned to Epworth but continued to correspond with her lover and expected to marry him.

However, while John appeared to have a high opinion of Leybourne, her brother, Sammy, did not share his views and was determined to disrupt the relationship. Emilia was stunned and the final blow came when her mother sent for her.

"This young man is not a fit person for you to marry, Emilia," Susanna told her bluntly. "And I must ask you to cease writing to him. There can be no future for you with him."

"But, Mama, I love him and he loves me," wailed her eldest daughter.

"That may be but I command you to obey me in this."

"Then I am resolved never to marry." Emilia was heartbroken. She was sure that Sammy had been instrumental in making her lose the one man she truly loved. But a woman of her times, she felt she could not disobey her mother. Unlike her younger sister, she needed her parents' blessing on her marriage but she became very bitter at losing her one

chance of happiness. Soon afterwards she went to Lincoln
to teach in a girls' boarding school.

Susanna missed her children—particularly the boys. She
was therefore delighted when Samuel suggested they should
take a boy from the Charity School into their home.

"Have you someone in mind?" she asked him.

"I have been watching Johnny Whitelamb from the
Wroot Charity School. I think he shows promise of being a
fine scholar. And he can help with carrying wood and
drawing water."

Susanna nodded. "I remember poor starveling Johnny.
I'm sure we can help him."

"And he can help us."

Samuel wasted no time and in 1723 Johnny Whitelamb
joined the household and became a popular member of it.
The Rector taught him Latin and Greek and let him tran-
scribe his continuing work on Job while Susanna treated him
like her own son.

The rift with her brother was causing her concern and she
wrote to him on her birthday January 20th 1722. She did not
mince her words although the letter was partly an attempt at
reconciliation but the feeling she had not long to live was
strong as was also her anger at the contents of her brother's
earlier letter.

Sir,

… feeling life ebb apace, and having a desire to be at
peace with all men, especially you, before my exit, I have
ventured to send one letter more, hoping you will give
yourself the trouble to read it without prejudice …

You say, 'I hope you have recovered your loss by fire long
since.' No; and it is to be doubted ever shall. Mr Wesley
rebuilt his house in less than a year, but nearly thirteen
years are elapsed since it was burned, yet it is not half
furnished nor his wife and children half clothed to this

day. It is true that the benefactions of his friends, to-gether with what he had himself, he paid the first; but the latter is not paid yet, or, what is much the same, money which was borrowed for clothes and furniture is yet unpaid.

You go on, 'My brother's living of £300 a year as they tell me.' *They?* Who? I wish those who say so were compelled to make it so. It may as truly be said that his living is £10,000 a year as £300. I have, Sir, previously laid before you the true state of our affairs. I have told you that the living was always let for £160 a year; that taxes, ... etc. took up nearly £30 of that, so that there needs no great skill in arithmetic to compute what remains.

Angrily, she continued to tell him the state of her household.

I am rarely in good health; Mr Wesley declines apace; my dear Emily, who in my present exigencies would exceed-ingly comfort me, is compelled to go to service in Lincoln, where she is a teacher in a boarding school; my second daughter, Sukey, a pretty woman and worthy a better fate, when by your last unkind letters, she perceived that all her hopes in you were frustrated, rashly threw herself upon a man (if a man he may be called who is little inferior to the apostate angels in wickedness) that is not only her plague but a great affliction to the family.

The other children, though wanting neither industry nor capacity for business, we cannot put to any, by reason we have neither money nor friends to assist us in doing it; neither is there a gentleman's family near us in which we can place them, unless as common servants, and that even yourself would not think them fit for, if you saw them ... Innumerable are other uneasinesses too tedious to mention; insomuch that with my own indisposition, my master's infirmities, the absence of my eldest, the ruin of my second daughter, and the inconceivable distress of all the rest, I have enough to turn a stronger heart than mine.[37]

It was unlike Susanna to give way to such anger and self pity and this letter shows the depths of despair to which she had sunk. Since she had married Samuel, she sometimes thought, nothing had gone right for them. But then she thought of her children and knew that she had done the best for them. After the letter to her brother had been sent, she tried not to think about him.

"I am sure he will be very angry with me and I shall never see him again," she thought sadly.

Letters to India took a considerable time to arrive so it would be months before she received a reply. Meanwhile her thoughts were given a new direction. In 1724 Samuel was offered the additional living of Wroot, a parish about five miles from Epworth.

"It will bring in an extra £50 a year, Sukey," her husband told her jubilantly. "We will move there and let this house. The parish and the parsonage at Wroot are smaller and our expenses will not be so high."

Susanna was practical. "But when the rains are excessive, there is no land link between the two. You will have to use a boat."

Samuel waved her objections aside. "So it would be if we remained here, my dear."

"Very well. I will write to tell Emilia to return home. I have but recently had a letter from her. She writes that the school is to close."

The move was accomplished fairly easily. However, the thatched parsonage was in dire need of repair.

"We shall have everything of the best, Sukey," Samuel announced. "I hear there is a good plumber and glazier in

---

37 Adam Clarke, *Memoirs of the Wesley Family*

the district, one William Wright. He can turn his hand to anything I am told."

"But we have no money for repairs, Samuel," replied his prudent wife.

"That is no matter. We shall not pay him immediately."

Susanna sighed. "Then we shall be yet more in debt."

Samuel ignored this and before long the house was filled with banging and clattering as William Wright installed a new larder, replaced the damaged fireplace in the parlour, inserted fresh lead in the window-casements and found yet more repairs to be done. Susanna felt some of them were not necessary but she knew it was pointless to argue.

When Samuel had engaged a curate to assist him at the cost of £30 a year, the family was no better off. Samuel was plunged more into debt and Emilia, who had consented to return, bitterly repented of her decision. She had enjoyed having money of her own but now she had no position, she could not stay in Lincoln.

Sitting in her room, huddled in a shawl against the bitter cold, she wrote to her brother John:

> I came home again in an evil hour for me. I was well clothed, and while I wanted nothing, was easy enough ... Thus far we went on tolerably well; but this winter, when my own necessaries began to decay, and my money was most of it spent (having maintained myself since I came home, but now could do it no longer), I found what condition I was in; every trifling want was either not supplied, or I had more trouble to procure it than it was worth. I know not when we have had so good a year, both at Wroot and at Epworth, as this year; but, instead of saving anything to clothe my sisters or myself, we are just where we were. A noble crop has almost all gone, beside Epworth living, to pay some part of those infinite debts my father has run into, which are so many, as I

have lately found out, that were he to save fifty pounds a year he would not be clear in the world this seven years.

Having relieved herself of her anxieties, she pondered on the blessings she and her family enjoyed:

Yet in this distress we enjoy many comforts. We have plenty of good meat and drink and fuel … [and have none] of that tormenting care for to provide bread which we had at Epworth. In short, could I lay aside all thought of the future, and could be content without three things, money, liberty, and clothes, I might live very comfortable. While my mother lives I am inclined to stay with her; she is so very good to me, and has so little comfort in the world besides, that I think it barbarous to abandon her.[38]

So Emilia remained at Wroot while her sister Sukey returned to Epworth. Samuel had rented it to the Ellisons. Susanna had not been happy about this as she knew Samuel found his son-in-law's bad language and domineering attitude to his wife hard to bear. But Ellison had money and promised to bring some order to his father-in-law's affairs so Samuel had to bow to the inevitable. Susanna was relieved that as she was at Wroot, she did not have to see much of Richard Ellison.

When her son, John wrote to his parents informing them he wished to follow his father into the Church and be ordained, she was delighted but to her surprise Samuel had reservations.

"He should take his time to decide," he informed his wife. "Meanwhile he should engage in further study. There is no harm to desire to get into that office but the principal spring and motive must certainly be the glory of God and the

---

38   Adam Clarke, *Memoirs of the Wesley Family*

service of His Church; woe to him who, with any meaner leading view, attempts so sacred a work."

"I am sure our son intends to bring glory to God by his desires," replied Susanna tartly. "I, at least, approve the disposition of his mind and think the sooner he is a deacon the better."

"Why do you always go against me, Sukey?" said Samuel sadly as he headed for the stairs and his study. "I shall write telling him of my views."

"And so shall I," retorted his wife.

In view of his closeness to her, it was not surprising it was his mother's advice John took and he started to prepare for his ordination. Susanna had tried not to think of her brother over the past few months and was therefore surprised when Samuel came into the parlour one evening waving a newspaper.

"I have news for you, Sukey."

She looked up from her sewing, smiling. "What is it?"

"Your brother is returning to England."

Susanna dropped her sewing and her eyes sit up. "Oh, when?"

Samuel referred to the paper. "He is listed as a passenger on the East Indiaman, the 'Albermarle' which docks in London next month."

"May I go to meet him? I should so like to see him again and I have not been to London since I left it over thirty years ago."

Samuel frowned. "You are not well, Sukey. It would be an arduous journey."

"It will be good for me to get away, Samuel. Surely you do not begrudge me a chance to see again my brother."

"Of course not. I have no doubt John will join you from Oxford if his finances allow it. And you will stay with Sammy and Ursula. I will write to my sons."

"I must start to prepare." Susanna bustled up. Her fatigue was forgotten and she looked forward with eager anticipation to seeing her brother again. Surely when she talked to him, all disagreements would be forgotten and he would provide financial help for her family as he had once promised.

The next few days were very busy for Susanna. Emilia took over the running of the house and Susanna concentrated on packing the few necessities she would need for her journey and for her sojourn in London.

The journey was long and arduous but in spite of her failing health, Susanna was eagerly anticipating meeting not only her brother but also her sons. This prospect kept up her spirits as the carriage bumped over the uneven roads and she tried to sleep in unfamiliar surroundings in a variety of inns. The journey took several days and as she neared London for the first time in thirty-four years, her excitement grew. She couldn't wait to visit the places where she had grown up. She stared eagerly out of the window of the carriage. People were everywhere — bustling about their business. Susanna smiled; she felt as though she were coming home. The carriage stopped outside her son's house and Samuel limped out to meet her. He had been ill with gout and his leg was very painful.

"How was the journey, mother?"

"It was tiring. I am very glad to be here. But how are you?" Her eyes looked at him with concern.

"I am recovering. I will have your luggage brought in."

Ursula bustled forward and kissed her. "How have you left your family at Epworth?"

"They are well, thank you." Susanna gave Ursula a fond look. She could sometimes be sharp but she had made Sammy happy and for that Susanna could forgive her anything. She was also grateful that Ursula had never objected to Samuel providing financial help for his struggling parents.

"You will take a dish of tea, Mother?"

It was a statement rather than a question and Susanna nodded. Tea was unheard of in Epworth. It was an expensive luxury but one which she had once tasted before in her father's house. Susanna smiled as she remembered the excitement when her father had first brought some home. It was still so expensive it had to be kept locked up.

The servant carried in the paraphernalia for the ritual of tea making and Susanna watched as her daughter-in-law carefully unlocked the tea caddy with a key from the bunch at her waist. She spooned a little tea into the tea pot, filled it with water from the hot water jug and then set it on the spirit lamp which she had lit. Susanna relaxed. The privations of Epworth seemed a world away from this elegant drawing room. She wondered how they were managing without her.

"Mother, your tea." Ursula held out a delicate china dish. There were no handles and Susanna took it gingerly. The hot, sweet beverage had a delicate flavour and it warmed her as she sipped it. She must not drink too much of it while she was in London as she knew it was a stimulant drug. Ursula handed her husband another dish.

"Has John not yet arrived from Oxford?" Susanna queried after she had taken several sips of the brew.

Ursula frowned. "He is not coming. He wrote that his finances are in a bad state so he did not feel he could come."

"Oh." Susanna was bitterly disappointed. She had so looked forward to seeing her favourite son and hearing his news. She had hoped they would be able to walk around London together.

"I'm so sorry, Mother." Ursula looked sympathetic. "I know how much you have longed to see him."

"No doubt God overruled." Susanna managed a brave smile. "Now dear, I should like to retire for a while. Perhaps you would show me to my room."

Samuel and Ursula exchanged glances. "Mother, we thought it better that you should stay with Uncle Matthew Wesley. He has room and is expecting you."

"Oh." Susanna frowned. She had been looking forward to staying with her son. "But he is a widower."

"He has an excellent housekeeper, Sally. She will look after you well. I will call a sedan chair for you and we will send your luggage later."

"Very well." Susanna followed him to the door and out into the street. A sedan chair was passing and he hailed it. Susanna climbed aboard while Sammy gave the front man directions. The journey was short and uncomfortable as sometimes the men were walking and sometimes running. She was relieved to arrive and to be greeted by the buxom housekeeper who bobbed her a curtsey.

"You are very welcome, Mrs Wesley. Mr Wesley is not yet back from his morning rounds. No doubt you wish to rest after your long journey."

"Thank you."

Susanna was grateful for the comfort of a soft bed with fresh clean linen sheets and she later enjoyed a better night's sleep than she had had for several days. Early the next morning her brother-in-law knocked at her door.

"The 'Albermarle' has entered the river, sister. You will be able to meet your brother today."

Susanna smiled happily. "Thank you brother. I will be down directly." Today she would see her beloved brother again and she was sure all the bitterness of the last few years would evaporate when they met face to face. But first she had another call to make. She knew Sammy was not well enough to walk with her but she could take her youngest son, Charles.

She made her way towards Westminster. About to enter Deans Yard, she was nearly knocked over by a young boy wearing a black gown. She recognised him as a King's Scholar, the same as her son.

"Sorry, ma'am." He rushed off and she gazed thoughtfully after him. A noise caught her ear and she followed the sound to find a group of boys cheering on two boys who had just finished what appeared to be the first round of a serious fight.

Susanna surveyed the scene. The shorter boy, thin, clear skinned and extremely good looking stepped forward to meet his challenger. She did not need a second glance to tell her it was her youngest son. Closing her eyes, she prayed that his opponent would not damage him too much. When she opened them, she saw that her son had drawn blood and had himself received a blow to his eye. She clenched her fists. How long would this go on. Suddenly Charles saw an opening. Plunging forward, he aimed several jabs at his opponent who moaned and collapsed on the turf. The cheering escalated and Charles grinned, making nonchalantly for his corner where he sponged his face and his bare chest clean of blood. The treatment of his eye would have to wait. His mother moved towards him.

"Let me do that for you." She held out her hand for the sponge. Charles looked up, startled, but smiled when he saw who it was. Shaking his head, he withdrew, his eyes warning her.

Quickly, she drew back, blushing. He was no longer her baby. He was a young man of seventeen. She had seen him only twice since he had left home for Westminster at the age of eight. He finished sponging himself and put on his shirt. Then he held out his hand to his mother.

"What brings you to London, Mother?"

"Will you walk with me to the Docks to meet your Uncle Samuel Annesley. He has but today returned from India."

"That is good news. We could take the boat from here."

"'Twill be cheaper to walk to Blackwall and take one there. I have very little money, Charles."

Her son felt embarrassed. He had forgotten their straitened circumstances. Together they walked to Matthew Wesley's house where Susanna was determined to treat her son's eye which was already showing signs of bruising.

"Master Charles requires a beefsteak for his eye, Sally," she informed the housekeeper.

Sally twinkled at the young man's embarrassment as she bustled away to find one. Having submitted to his mother's ministrations, Charles had to admit his eye felt less painful. When she was satisfied with her treatment, Susanna and her son continued to walk towards the Docks. As they neared their destination, the roads became busier and they had to dodge the wagons piled high with goods going to and from the Docks. Sometimes they had to avoid porters trundling barrels out of the warehouses which lined the route.

At last they reached Blackwall Stairs where Susanna halted and caught her breath. "Look, Charles," she gasped. "There are two Indiaman docked. One of them must be the 'Albermarle' on which your uncle sailed."

Charles shaded his eyes with his hand. "One of them is weighing anchor. How beautiful she is. Look how gracefully she moves away."

Susanna was already bargaining with a drunken waterman. "I will give you threepence to row us across to the 'Albermarle'", she said, "and not a penny more."

"You drive a hard bargain, lady," growled the man as Charles helped his mother descend the steps and climb into the small boat. Halfway across, the boatman stopped and demanded more money but a steely look from the lady's eyes forced him to bend angrily to his oars again.

"You had best ship your oar if you do not want it broken," said Susanna placidly as the huge Indiaman towered over them. He glared at her and a moment later his oar snapped and he was hurled back. There was a roar of laughter from above and Susanna looked up to see a crowd of grinning sailor lads.

"I should like to see your captain," she called.

One of them shouted down to her, "If you'll come aboard ma'am, I'll take you to him."

"Thank you."

One of the lads came down the ship's ladder to assist her and Charles clambered up behind her. They followed their guide down the slippery deck; Susanna held up her skirts to avoid the damp boards while Charles strode along behind her. The boy stopped in front of a door.

"Here, ma'am. This is Captain Bewes' office."

"Thank you." Taking a deep breath, she knocked at the door.

"Enter."

Her hand trembling, she opened the door and stepped into a bare room containing a bunk bed and a desk on which were strewn a number of papers. In front of it sat a well proportioned man of about fifty. When he saw her, he leapt to his feet, looking astonished.

"Can I help you, ma'am? Pray take a seat."

He waved her to the chair he had just vacated and she sank down gratefully. She had been standing for a long time and her legs were shaking with apprehension. Charles stood beside her, looking round with interest.

"I wish to know if—if Mr Samuel Annesley sailed with you. I believe he did and so I assume he must be still on board. Could you take me to him, Sir?"

She raised her eyes to him and he thought what a good looking woman she was in spite of the tiredness that had etched lines on her pale face. What was he to tell her? He was still bewildered by the turn of events. He played for time.

"You are — a kinswoman of his, ma'am?"

"He is my brother, Sir."

"Ah."

She gazed at him and waited for him to continue but he did not. He looked extremely embarrassed. What could be wrong? Her heart fluttered.

"Is—is he ill, Sir? We read in the newspaper he had taken passage with you."

"Why so he did, ma'am. To the best of my knowledge he sailed with us."

"Then where is he?" cried Susanna. "What has happened? Why will you not tell me?"

The captain cleared his throat. "Well ma'am. It is a very grave situation. We do not understand it at all. The fact of the matter is — Mr Annesley could not be found when we docked. He — he has disappeared, ma'am."

"Disappeared?" Susanna felt as though she would faint.

Hurriedly, the captain found his ever present bottle of rum and poured a little into his pewter tankard. "Here take a little of this." He handed it to her.

"No. No. I am quite all right. Thank you. I — er — are you *sure* he has disappeared?"

"I'm afraid so, ma'am. I'm very sorry. Perhaps you would like to see his cabin."

Susanna shook her head. "No—no thank you. You have been very kind. I must go." She stood up and looked at him. "No doubt you will do whatever needs to be done."

"You can rest assured of that, ma'am. Where can I contact you if there is any news?"

Susanna recovered her wits. She wanted to learn as much about her brother as possible. "Perhaps, Sir, you would like to sup with us tonight. I am lodging with my brother-in-law, Mr Matthew Wesley, the apothecary, in Johnson's Court. You would be very welcome and I should like to hear whatever you can tell me of my brother."

"You are very kind, ma'am. I should be delighted to join you." She gave him directions and then turned and walked away with Charles following her.

"Come, Mother." Her son stepped forward and took her arm. He guided her back to the ladder and helped her down into another boat that was waiting there. This time the waterman did not argue about the price. As they turned from the docks, dark clouds obscured the sun and Susanna's feet felt leaden. She leant heavily on her son.

"What can have happened to him? Surely foul play must be suspected although Captain Bewes did not say so. Your uncle was a wealthy man."

"Did—did we have expectations, mother?"

"Yes — once we did. He lead me to believe I would receive one thousand pounds."

Charles gasped. Such riches were unimaginable. They walked the rest of the way in silence. Susanna had been buoyed up by the excitement of meeting her brother and now that her hopes had been dashed, she was exhausted.

"I must get back now, Mother," Charles said as he left her at his uncle's door.

"Very well, dear. Thank you for accompanying me." Matthew was not home so she went wearily to her room to rest before supper.

Later that evening the family gathered round the supper table to hear Captain Bewes' story. He was worried too. To lose such a valued passenger would not endear him to the East India Company for whom he had worked for many years. He hoped to convince the family that he was not to blame for whatever had happened.

Matthew Wesley sat at the head of the table and alternately puffed at his pipe and sipped at his glass of hot rum and sugar. Sugar had now replaced honey as a sweetener and rum was distilled from the sugar cane harvested in the West Indies. As a seaman, Captain Bewes was no stranger to it and delighted to be able to sip it to give him courage to tell his story.

"Before we sailed, I was sitting in my stateroom which lay beside Mr Annesley's cabin. The three windows were open behind me for air. It was very hot and I knew we were nearly ready to sail. Mr Orchard, my second mate, knocked at the door to tell me all was ready to cast off. As he said this, there was a splash just outside my window. Both of us moved quickly to look through the window but we could see nothing."

He paused and Matthew took his pipe out of his mouth to ask, "Nothing at all?"

"Nothing at all, Sir. It could have been any one of a dozen things, rubbish being heaved overboard, one of the ropes getting loose and striking the water. I thought no more of it until the next day when we found Mr Annesley's cabin empty."

"You did not miss him immediately you sailed then?" Susanna was frowning.

"No ma'am. It is quite usual for gentlemen to keep to themselves at first. There was no reason to enter his cabin. But when we found he was missing, Mr Orchard told me that after leaving my stateroom the previous day, he had seen an old Hindu beggar crouching at the door of Mr Annesley's cabin. Mr Orchard said his hand was on the handle as if he intended to enter. He did not succeed as Mr Orchard kicked him off the boat."

"So you think this beggar may have been involved in my brother's disappearance." Susanna was still suffering from shock at what had happened.

"Who is to say, ma'am? I cannot tell but I felt I should tell you all I know. The beggar man was frail and of a great age. I think he could not have pushed an active man like Mr Annesley through a cabin window. But your brother, ma'am, was known as a stern man. 'Tis likely he made many enemies during the time he was in India and Hindus are known for bearing grudges. There was no sign of the beggar the next day and when we broke into the cabin, our passenger could not be found. His boxes had not been unpacked and the cabin was as neat as a pin — apart from the handful of coins flung on to the bunk. It looked as though he had just emptied his pockets when he was interrupted."

"But if the beggar had entered the cabin, surely he would have taken the money," objected Sammy who was sitting facing the Captain with his injured leg propped on a footstool.

Captain Bewes shook his head. "They are not thieves, Sir. They are religious men who beg for alms believing that the money given blesses the giver."

"A strange race," remarked Matthew.

"It seems to me," said Susanna thoughtfully, "that the key to the mystery lies back in India. From his letters I am aware he had powerful enemies. I do not think he could have been kidnapped off a ship in broad daylight."

Captain Bewes stared at her as her meaning penetrated. "You suggest he may have decided it prudent to disappear to avoid his enemies."

"Nonsense!" exclaimed Matthew. "He would never have left his fortune behind."

The Captain rose to his feet. "His boxes shall be delivered to you tomorrow. I trust this mystery will soon be cleared up. Mr Wesley, I thank you for your hospitality. Your servant, ma'am." He bowed to Susanna and left the room.

"I think we shall never know what has happened to my brother," said Susanna, sadly. She was right. Samuel Annesley was never heard of again. Repeated enquiries failed to uncover the mystery of his disappearance and his fortune vanished with him.[39]

---

39   Some details of the above account are taken from *Hetty Wesley* by Sir Arthur Quiller-Couch

CHAPTER NINE

Hetty Elopes

Dejected and weary, Susanna made the long journey back to Wroot to face yet more problems. During the early part of 1725 a smallpox epidemic raged in the parish. It was worse than the one of 1711 and on this occasion, of the family who were at home at the time, all succumbed except Susanna herself. She had hoped that those who had had the disease earlier would have been immune from it but it was not to be and Susanna wore herself out soothing fevered brows and trying to calm the distraught patients. Fortunately all the family survived and Susanna's treatment once again proved effective as none of her offspring retained the disfiguring marks of this dreaded disease.

Susanna's troubles were not over. Her husband was becoming frailer and in the spring he had a slight stroke and lost the use of his right hand. This was a blow but he bore it with fortitude.

"I have lost one hand," he told his wife a few days later, "but I have begun to put my left hand to school this day to write in order to help its lame brother." He persevered and became quite proficient at writing with his left hand.

Meanwhile, Hetty, their fourth daughter, was causing problems for her parents. Beautiful as she was, she attracted a variety of suitors, most of whom would not have made suitable husbands for this lively girl. Hetty knew this but she objected strongly to her father's interference. She was irritated by his authoritarian dictates and one day in frustration, she wrote a poem to her mother pleading with her to play the mediator between her and her father.

> Pray speak a word in time of need
> And with my sour-look'd father plead
> For your distressed daughter![40]

This did not seem to have any effect and Samuel continued to disapprove of all her suitors. She enjoyed their attentions but had never yet fallen in love with any of them. But because of her father's persistent interference, this was to change. In Wroot she met John Romley, the schoolmaster. For a short time he was also Samuel's curate and he became deeply attached to Hetty. She was not interested in him but was flattered by his attentions.

One evening early in 1725 the Ellisons and Romley were invited to the Rectory at Wroot. John Wesley was also staying in the house at the time. John Romley, who was known to have a fine singing voice was asked to entertain the company with a song.

Unfortunately he chose to sing the satirical song, 'The Vicar of Bray'. Samuel became angrier and angrier as he listened to the account of the fictitious vicar who changed his doctrine to suit the views of whichever monarch was on the throne at the time. In this way he hoped to gain the good will of the sovereign and thus gain preferment.

The end of the song was greeted by restrained applause by the Wesley family, raucous laughter from the uncouth

---

40   Adam Clarke, *Memoirs of the Wesley Family*

Ellison and fury from the Rector who felt it had been aimed at him.

"You insult me, Sir," he shouted. "I will not have such things sung in my house. You will leave, Sir. Immediately."

Romley was bewildered. He had merely meant to entertain and had had no thought of insulting Hetty's father. But his days as a suitor were numbered. Samuel had determined that Romley was not a suitable husband for his beautiful, intelligent daughter.

The next day he went to visit a wealthy family the Granthams in the village of Kelstern, a few miles away. Then he sent for his wayward daughter.

"Hetty, John Romley is *not* a suitable husband for you. You deserve the best. I will not have you throwing yourself away on this, this — ." Words failed him and Hetty opened her mouth to agree with him. She had no intention of marrying Romley. But before she could say anything, he was off again. "You have been nothing but trouble since you were born. You are wilful, disobedient and rebellious and I can no longer tolerate this. I have arranged for you to go to Mr and Mrs Grantham in Kelstern to be governess to their two young children. I have told Mrs Grantham that you do not need to be paid."

"But father … " Hetty had never expected to be sent away in disgrace. Then it occurred to her that she was not averse to being away from the strict regime at Wroot for a while. Yes, it would suit her very well even though she would apparently be penniless. She smiled demurely at the angry man in front of her. "Very well, father, I am happy to obey you."

Susanna was sorry to say good-bye to her wayward daughter but she, too, thought it was for the best. As things turned out, Hetty's banishment to Kelstern merely created more problems. Soon after she arrived, she was introduced to a young lawyer named Will Attkins[41]. For the first time Hetty fell head over heels in love. Her love was reciprocated and she floated around with her head in the clouds.

They met whenever they could and Will planned delightful surprises for her. One of these misfired. They had been skating on the canal and reached a secluded place where Will had planned a picnic. Nearby was an old barge frozen into the water. On its deck stood a woman who was glowering at a man who was hammering at a kettle.

The woman dropped a curtsey when they appeared. "Sorry to keep you waiting, Sir. The dish of tea should have been ready for the young lady if it hadn't been for this lazy wretch here."

The man looked up and met Hetty's eyes. He grinned. Her heart sank. It was the plumber from Wroot, William Wright.

"Well now, ain't this a surprise? If I'd known it was Miss Wesley I was doin' it for, I'd 'ave hurried meself a bit."

Hetty's companion glared at him. "Do you know this fellow, Hetty?"

Before she could answer, the man broke into a raucous guffaw. "Sure she knows me. Shall I tell the Rector, Miss, what company you keep?"

Will stepped forward and Hetty grabbed his arm alarmed at his expression. "Leave it Will. Let's go."

Scowling, he followed her but the day had been spoiled and they skated back in silence. William Wright watched them. One day his knowledge of the behaviour of the Rector's beautiful daughter might be useful.

---

41   Hetty refused to name her lover so there are no records to
       support this name but he seems the most likely candidate.

Hetty returned to her post to be met by an irate Mrs Grantham. "Where have you been, Hetty? You were needed."

Hetty bit her lip. "I have been skating on the canal, Mrs Grantham. It is such a lovely day."

Her employer gave her a sour look. "I wish to speak with you. Come in here."

Hetty followed her into the parlour and stood awkwardly, her skates still dangling from her hand. She had never been happy in her situation; she knew Mrs Grantham did not like her and had only agreed to take her because of Samuel's persuasion. Now the lady no longer had any need of Hetty's services.

"Your father desired me to take you and I did not know well how to refuse him," Mrs Grantham told her bluntly. "But come May Day you must provide for yourself."

Hetty did not want to return home but when, in April, Will Attkins proposed to her, she decided to do the right thing. They both journeyed to Wroot to ask Samuel for his blessing on their marriage. Samuel, meanwhile, had been told about Hetty's latest infatuation by Mrs Grantham. Still determined that nothing but the best would do for his beautiful daughter he investigated the young man's background and was not impressed with what he discovered.

"I will not give my consent to your marriage to my daughter," he told the young man firmly. "And now I wish you to leave my house and never to see Hetty again."

When Hetty came into the study, Will had already left. Hetty stared at her father in horror.

"But why, father?" she asked. "Why have you sent Will away? I want to marry him. He loves me."

"He is an unprincipled lawyer," Samuel stormed at her. "He has a frivolous attitude towards life and he is not good enough for you. He will let you down."

"But father, I love him. I've never loved anyone else and I never will. I want to marry him and he wants to marry me. Please give us your blessing."

"I will not have you throwing yourself away on that worthless young man. You would not be happy, Hetty. I know it and I forbid you to see him again."

Hetty's mind was racing and her heart pounding. For once she was determined to stand up to her father. It was, after all, he from whom she had inherited her obstinate streak.

"Father, I am twenty seven. I am quite old enough to make up my own mind. I love Will and I am determined to marry him."

She turned to leave and her father shouted, "If you marry him, I will never see you again. You will be barred from this house. Do you wish to break your mother's heart?"

Hetty hesitated but her mind was made up. How her marriage was to be achieved without her father's consent, she was not sure but at that moment she was as angry as he was. She went to find her mother and her anger culminated in a burst of furious weeping.

"You cannot go against your father, child," said Susanna gently as she laid her hand on the dark head. "He is the head of this household and you must obey him. That is the way of things."

"But I love Will," wailed Hetty.

"There will be others. Soon you will find a suitable young man to love and marry. Your father only wants the best for you."

"I know but I can't give up Will." Hetty lifted her tearstained face to her mother. "I don't know what to do."

"You must give him up, Hetty. Your father says he is not worthy of you."

"He'll say that about anyone I want to marry," muttered Hetty rebelliously.

She wandered out of the house and over the fields. It was early May and the sun was warm. She was sure Will had not gone far away and they would be able to make some plans. She was right.

"Hetty." Will stepped out from behind a bush.

"Oh Will." Hetty flung herself into his arms. "What are we going to do?"

Will held her tightly. "Don't worry, my love. I have it all planned. We will elope."

"Elope!" gasped Hetty. She pulled herself away and stared at him, scandalised.

"What else can we do, my dear. You wish to marry me, don't you?"

"You know I do." Hetty's brain was reeling but now her eyes had lit up. Of course eloping was the only thing to do. When they were safely married, her father was bound to relent when he saw what a splendid husband Will was. She squeezed her lover's arm. "Tell me what to do."

"I'll buy a special marriage licence so we can be married as soon as possible. Can you be ready to leave now."

"Now?" Hetty thought for a moment. She would be very sad to leave her family but what alternative did she have? The sooner she was married, the sooner the reconciliation could take place. "Have I time to pack a few things?"

"I'll bring some horses. Meet me here in an hour."

Hetty nodded and waved to Will as she skipped home to make plans to defy her father in a way for which he would never forgive her. After packing a few necessities, she left a note for her mother and crept out of the house without being seen. She hurried to the meeting place and found Will waiting for her holding two docile horses. Soon they were on their way. In the exhilaration and excitement of the moment she forgot the heartache she would cause her mother who would have to bear the brunt of her father's wrath.

They travelled across country for several hours and as the sun disappeared over the horizon, they reached Lincoln. They found a lodging house where they could stay and Will followed Hetty into the bedroom. She blushed.

"Do they not have two rooms, Will? It is not right for you to be here with me."

"But tomorrow we will be married, dearest Hetty. What difference will one night make?"

Hetty hesitated but when he moved towards her and took her in his arms, her resistance crumbled.

"I must go out now, dearest," he told her. "When I return, we will have supper."

"You go to get the licence. Oh Will." Hetty remembered something. "John Romley, who was curate for a time at Wroot, is now at the Cathedral. He hopes to be the precentor. He will help us, I am sure. He could marry us tomorrow."

Will smiled and kissed her. It was late when he returned and Hetty had already been given a serving of nourishing potato pudding and a small glass of wine by the landlady. She had been hungry as she had eaten nothing all day so was grateful to eat the repast in her room.

When Will came home, she thought he had been drinking but he was very loving to her.

"You are so late, Will. Shall I ask for something to be sent up? I have already eaten."

"I have had something. Come dearest." He led her to the bed and overcoming her scruples, she enjoyed a night of bliss with her lover — possibly the last few hours of happiness she was ever to know. Her bubble of bliss burst into a thousand fragments the next day.

She woke to find her prospective bridegroom hurriedly packing. It was still dark.

"Must we leave now?" she asked sleepily. "Where are we to be married?"

He turned, startled. "Go back to sleep, my love. I have to go out."

A chill crept over Hetty. "Can I not come?"

"No."

"When will you be back?"

"Soon." Hurriedly kissing her, he left. She had forgotten to ask him about the licence but assumed he had seen Romley and that the wedding was all arranged. She lay in bed for a while longer and then got up. It grew light but there was no sign of her lover. His bag lay neatly packed in the corner. She dressed hurriedly expecting any moment to hear his footsteps but he did not come. Having peered out of the window for the hundredth time, she hurriedly pulled her cape round her and tiptoed down the stairs. She did not want to meet the landlady and face her questioning eyes.

She heard the Cathedral clock chime eight o'clock and hurried towards it. She must find John Romley. He would know what was happening. Will must have seen him. Perhaps *he* had the licence. Struggling up Steep Hill, she breathed heavily. By the time she reached the Cathedral, the weekday service had started and she slipped into a pew dropping forward to kneel. But she could not pray. Her brain was churning and her heart pounding — not only because she was out of breath.

Gradually she became aware of a familiar voice echoing around the arches and addressing the few worshippers scattered in front of the great pulpit. Raising her head, she gazed at John Romley. She knew how much he wanted to be the precentor but he was still on trial. He had a beautiful voice, she reflected, but she was in no mood to listen to what he was saying. She was too impatient for the service to end so she could talk to him. She looked around at the minute congregation. There was no sign of Will. Perhaps he had returned to the lodging house and was wondering what had become of her.

At last the service ended and she moved to the porch knowing that Romley would have to leave by the main entrance. She did not have long to wait before he hurried through the door carrying his robes.

"Mr Romley." She touched his arm and he looked round, startled.

"Miss—Miss Hetty! What a pleasant surprise to find you in Lincoln. I must call upon your father. I trust he has forgiven me for my song. I look to his support in my application to the Cathedral. Where are you staying?"

"My father is not with me. I came upon a different matter. Oh Mr Romley, you have the licence, do you not?"

He looked bewildered. "Licence? What licence?"

"The marriage licence. Will and I are to be wed. Oh John, say you have it and you will come and marry us."

He stared at her. "Marry you ... to him? My dear Hetty, what can you be thinking of? Of course I can do no such thing. I have no licence for you. I do not understand you."

Hetty was nearly crying. Had she made a terrible mistake? "But you must. It is all arranged. I thought you would have the licence but Will must have it. Please come with me so it will be all right."

He could not refuse her although he was desperately afraid of jeopardising his chances of become the precentor. He followed her down Steep Street. The traders had opened their shops and were plying their trade. Behind one grimy window a man in a baize apron sat at a bench working. He looked up as the couple passed. Then hurriedly removing his apron, William Wright left the shop and followed them.

What was she doing with the young man who had been thrown out of the vicarage?

When the couple reached the lodging house, Romley looked around him with distaste. This was not the type of place he would have expected to find the fastidious Miss Wesley. But she seemed unaware of her surroundings and of the giggling of the landlady and the maid as she led her companion into the parlour.

Will was seated behind the table draining a pewter tankard. He had obviously breakfasted well and opposite him a place had been laid for Hetty. But she had no interest in food at that moment.

"Will, here is John Romley. I have brought him here to marry us. You have the licence?"

Two pairs of eyes stared at her. Will scowled. "Why have you brought him here?"

"To marry us, of course. I made sure you had given him the licence so I went to find him. But *you* must have it. Please give it to me. John will need it."

"I want no parson here."

She stared at him. her cheeks gradually whitening. "You have not got the licence?"

He looked embarrassed. "I have had no time," he muttered.

"You have not got it? You have not even applied for it." The full horror of what had happened finally penetrated her numbed brain. "You — you never intended — oh what have you done to me. You have ruined me."

Her voice ended in a wail and carried outside the window to William Wright who gave a small grunt of satisfaction. The Rector still owed him money for the repairs to the rectory at Wroot. Perhaps he would be willing to bargain. His thoughts busy, he moved away before he could be seen.

Inside the room John Romley had dropped the robes he was clutching and had moved swiftly towards Hetty's lover.

"You — you scoundrel!" Before Will realised what was happening, John had hit him. Will gazed, bemused at the blood streaming from his nose but made no attempt to retaliate. Hetty screamed and John recollected himself.

"I beg your pardon, Miss Hetty. That was unpardonable of me."

She was white and dazed. "I must go home."

"Let me find you a carriage."

"No — thank you. Just let me go."

Running out of the room, she ignored the landlady who had been listening at the door, and ran down the street. She must get as far away from Lincoln and her shame as she could. She walked and walked until her feet were swollen and bleeding. But the time she had covered the ten miles to Marton, she was exhausted and grateful to accept a lift in a carriage containing a family on a day trip to Gainsborough. They were friendly but Hetty was too tired to talk.

At Gainsborough she started to walk again but soon a farmer transporting a wagon load of hay took pity on her.

"I'm going to Haxey, lass. Tha' looks as though tha' could do with a ride."

"Thank you," gasped Hetty clambering aboard. Haxey was only about five miles from Wroot. Surely she would be able to manage to walk the last stretch.

As she crossed the fields towards the Rectory, her control broke and she started to sob. What sort of reception would she receive?

As she neared the Rectory, she slowed and her sobbing increased. Would she be allowed to remain at Wroot? Her father was so stubborn and he had been right about Will. Why hadn't she listened to him? But *she* had had no warning of his true character. He had always been charming and loving. He had given her no reason to believe he meant to renege on his promise to marry her.

She walked slowly to the front door. Smoke was drifting out of the chimney and she knew both her parents were early risers. Raising her hand, she knocked at the door.

If flew open and to her horror, it was her father who stood there. He glared at her, taking in her crumpled clothes and tearstained face.

"Father," she faltered.

"You're no daughter of mine," he thundered. "Left you, has he? I warned you he was unprincipled but you wouldn't listen. You've ruined not only your own reputation but you have stained the honour of the Wesleys and the Annesleys. How could you let us down so?"

She heard the hurt pride in her father's voice and for the first time realised the extent of her guilt and felt pity for him. For the carefully brought up daughter of a highly respected clergyman to behave in such a way had brought shame on her whole family. She was not the only one who would suffer.

"May I not come in, Father?" she begged. "I am truly sorry for my sin."

"I will not have such a wanton under my roof. Go girl and find lodgings elsewhere."

"Samuel!" Susanna swept out of the kitchen. "She has repented. Should not a Christian show forgiveness? She is your daughter. You cannot turn her from your door."

"I can and I will. She is no daughter of mine."

Susanna was as stubborn as he was. "She is my daughter too. I will not have her turned out of doors."

Samuel turned his back on her. "Do what you like," he shouted, "but don't expect me to speak to her."

Susanna looked sorrowfully at her erring daughter. "Oh Hetty," she sighed. "Why did you not listen to your father?"

"He always interferes. Why can't I lead my own life?" Some of Hetty's rebelliousness returned.

"He only wants what is best for you."

"Even now?"

"He is angry." Susanna took her daughter's arm. "Come child. You are chilled and tired. Sit by the fire and drink some broth. Then you must go and rest. I hope your father will relent."

It was soon obvious that Samuel had no intention of communicating with his daughter and he never became reconciled to her. Something else also became apparent to Hetty in the following weeks. She was pregnant! Desperate, she searched for a way out. Eventually, miserable at her father's rejection, the lack of sympathy shown by the rest of her family and the bleak life stretching ahead of her, she made a decision.

Startling her family, one meal time, she announced, "I vow that I will marry the first man who asks me."

There was a shocked silence. Only Molly, her crippled sister, had shown kindness to her and it was she who spoke first. "That is not a proper vow to make, sister Hetty. You will regret it."

"Marriage to anyone would be better than the life I am forced to live here. I've made my vow, sister Molly, and I mean to stand by it." She pushed back her chair and ran out of the room.

Molly shook her head sadly, "Oh father, can't you find it in your heart to forgive Hetty. She is so unhappy."

"She has shown no true repentance. She thinks only of herself. I hope she soon finds herself a husband. I shall certainly make her keep her vow."

He was given his opportunity a few days later. William Wright, the plumber, who had dogged Hetty's path for the past year, had been biding his time. He had always been attracted to the beautiful, wayward Wesley girl but knew that in the normal course of events, he would have no hope of winning her. However, Hetty had now ruined her reputation and he was determined to chance his luck.

Early one morning he arrived at the Rectory demanding to see the Rector. He was taken upstairs and ushered into the Rector's study. John Whitelamb looked up in disapproval.

"I'm here to see the Rector on a matter of business. William Wright's the name and I come now from Lincoln."

"You had best leave us, John."

"Yes Mr Wesley." Whitelamb gathered up his papers and left.

"You have come about your payment no doubt, Mr Wright. I believe it was twelve pounds, seventeen shillings and sixpence. I'm afraid it is extremely awkward for me to pay it just now. Perhaps — er — perhaps you would not mind waiting a little longer."

"I never said I wanted payment, Sir."

"Oh? Then why have you come?"

The plumber mopped his face with a dingy red handkerchief. What he had to say was not easy. "Has Miss Hetty come back?" he croaked.

The Rector looked surprised. "Yes she has but I fail to see what business it is of yours."

"I saw her in Lincoln. I followed her and saw her with that … Well I knew she was seeing him and I …"

"Mr Wright!" Samuel's leapt out of his chair. His well known temper was rising to the surface. "You forget yourself."

"No, Sir. Begging your pardon, Sir. 'Tis a bad business, Sir. What are you going to do about her?"

"Do about … ?" Words failed the Rector as he gazed at the other man.

William hastened on. "Well, Sir, I warned the young lady about 'im but she took no notice and now … Well Sir, here's my point. She's beautiful and accomplished and she makes me feel like dirt. But I — I — worship her, Sir. And now, Sir, she's fallen off her perch so to speak and no man will look at her." He paused and dared to raise his eyes to Hetty's father. "You understand me, Mr Wesley?"

"To my sorrow I do, Sir, but...." The Rector slumped back in his chair.

"Well, Sir, as I said, I do worship Miss Hetty and 'ave done ever since I first set eyes on 'er and …"

"Knowing her conduct, you wish to marry my daughter, Mr Wright?" Samuel interrupted.

William swallowed. "Yes, Sir," he muttered.

Samuel Wesley stared at the man before him. Then he picked up a small handbell and rang it. After a moment, the door opened and Susanna appeared.

"My dear, this honest plumber from Lincoln has just offered to marry Hetty."

Susanna gasped and turned her incredulous gaze upon William. "Marry Hetty!" she echoed.

"In view of the circumstances, I consider his offer a most generous one."

"But Samuel … " Susanna tightened her lips. She could hardly argue in front of their visitor.

Samuel stood up. "Return tomorrow, Sir, and I shall give you my answer."

William bowed and left hurriedly. He could not believe that the Rector had not thrown him out for his presumption.

As soon as he had gone, Susanna rounded on her husband. "Samuel, we cannot possibly let Hetty marry that man. He is not worthy of her."

"She vowed to marry the first honest man who would take her."

"You have no right to bind her to such a vow. It makes my flesh creep to think of him and Hetty together."

"She has gone her own way. We have other children to consider. I will no longer harbour such a wanton in my house."

Susanna hurried from the room, hiding her tears from her husband. She knew Hetty had gone for a walk and she set out to warn her of her fate. She found her daughter standing by a gate staring sadly over the fields.

"Hetty." Her mother gently touched her arm.

Dully Hetty turned to her. "A man passed me just now. I hoped it was—Will. But it was not. It was the plumber who is owed money. I suppose he came to be paid."

"Do you know much of him?"

"Of the plumber. No." Hetty turned to look at her mother. A chill crept through her veins. "What did he want, Mother?"

"He has told your father he will marry you. He is to come for his answer tomorrow. I told your father it is impossible but I fear he will not listen to me."

Hetty's pale face became even whiter. "I made a vow," she whispered.

"Your father has no right to hold you to it."

"But he will—won't he?"

Susanna bowed her head. "Oh my dearest child, I am very much afraid he will."

Hetty was already repenting of her rash vow. How could she possibly marry a man like William Wright after her handsome Will?

But the Rector was adamant. The next day she was called to his study and faced her parents and her prospective bridegroom. Her father looked stern but her mother was sad and had been weeping.

The Rector wasted no words. "You have asked to marry my daughter, Mr Wright. She is in no position to refuse you so I agree to the marriage."

William looked embarrassed. "Thank you, Sir," he muttered. "But I should like to hear what Miss Hetty says."

Hetty looked straight at the man who was to make her so unhappy. "I have made a vow and if my father will not release me from it, I must marry you."

"I will not release you," stated Samuel.

"Then Sir, I will try to be a good wife to you." She held out her hand to the plumber and his dirty fingers touched hers gently. Then she dropped a brief curtsey to her parents and left. She was already repenting of her rash vow. Her future husband was a drunkard, he associated with low company and they had nothing to say to one another.

"You can't marry him, sister Hetty," protested Molly. "He is not a fit husband for you."

"I know it," Hetty replied sadly. "But I fear I will not be allowed to break my vow. Would I had never made it."

"Father must release you from it and prevent you marrying William Wright. I will speak to him."

Molly did so but had to report failure. "He is adamant. Mama too has spoken to him but failed to move him."

"So I am to be sacrificed for my folly. I exchange one unhappy life for another."

Meanwhile her brother, John, had continued with his studies and both parents were proud of their son when on Sunday 19th September 1725 he was ordained deacon in Christ Church Cathedral in Oxford. He was twenty-two. The ceremony was performed by Dr John Potter, Bishop of Oxford.

Hetty married William Wright the following month on 13th October in the parish Church at Haxey. The Reverend Joseph Hoole officiated and afterwards the couple went to live in nearby Louth.

Another wedding took place on 2nd December. On that day Anne—or Nancy as she was called—married John Lambert, an Epworth land surveyor. She had been engaged to him for some time. He was well educated, came from a respectable family and was doing well in his work. For once Samuel was happy with his daughter's choice. He had even provided her with a respectable dowry although he had to incur more debts to do so. Susanna was glad that at least one of her daughters was not marrying in haste and hoped Nancy would not have to 'repent at leisure'.

"I think she will be happy," she said to Samuel, the night before the wedding.

"As long as he does not indulge his weakness for drink," rejoined her husband.

"Oh I do hope not," said Susanna, distressed. "I would like at least one of my daughters to be happy in her marriage."

Now that John had been ordained, he was able to assist his father at Wroot. Feeling that the Rector was showing a lack of Christian charity to her erring sister, Hetty, he prepared a sermon on 'universal charity'. When he showed it to his mother, she commented wryly, "You wrote this sermon for Hetty. You will offend your father."

John refused to change his subject. When his father heard the sermon, he flew into one of his famous tempers. He had no doubt as to John's meaning. Far from softening his feelings towards his daughter, it further exasperated them.

"I regard her with the utmost detestation," he snapped at Susanna when she tried to calm him. "And I intend to go and tell her so. She has disgraced her family and I shall never forgive her."

"No Samuel," gasped his horrified wife. "If you cannot forgive her, it is unkind of you to wound her further. She has suffered enough. Leave her alone now."

"My conscience will not let me rest until I have unburdened my mind to her. I must go, Sukey."

Nothing that Susanna or John could say would dissuade him and he angrily set off for Louth. He did not stay long and his anger had not abated when he returned. Susanna glanced anxiously at him as he strode into the kitchen. She dared not ask him how he had fared.

He answered her unspoken question. "I did not see her," he growled. "She was brought to bed two days before I arrived."

Susanna was relieved but she was sad for her daughter. She knew Hetty was not happy. She tried to be a 'good wife' but it was difficult because William started to drink heavily. He spent his evenings with unsavoury companions in taverns instead of with his wife. On one occasion the Lamberts, who had settled in Epworth, visited the Wrights at Louth. During the visit William encouraged John to engage in a heavy bout of drinking. Fortunately he was ashamed of himself afterwards and tried in the future, fairly successfully, to overcome his addiction. Nancy did not, therefore, suffer from the marital difficulties of her sisters Sukey and Hetty.

Early in the new year Hetty's baby died. It had lived only a few months and was buried at Louth on February 18th 1726. Hetty desperately missed her family at this time and eventually she plucked up courage to visit Wroot. Susanna and Molly were pleased to see her but their welcome was rather restrained.

"Your father will not forgive you, Hetty," said Susanna sadly. "I fear he will not see you."

"Oh Mother, I long for his forgiveness. I am truly sorry for my sin. Will you not speak to him?"

"I have tried my child. He will not be moved."

Hetty stayed for two days but returned to Louth without seeing her father. She had three more children who all died and after she lost the last one, she wrote in desperation to her father:

Honoured Sir,

Although you have cast me off, and I know that a determination once taken by you is not easily moved, I must tell you that some word of your forgiving is not only necessary to me but would make happier the marriage in which, as you compelled it, you must still, I think, feel no small concern. My child, on whose frail help I had counted to make our life more supportable to my husband and myself, is dead. Should God give and take away another, I can never escape the thought that my father's intercession might have prevailed against His wrath which I shall then, alas, take to be manifest …

As you planted my matrimonial bliss, so you cannot run away from my prayer when I beseech you to water it with a little kindness … I have come to a point where I feel your forgiveness to be necessary to me. I beseech you, then, not to withhold it.[42]

---

42   Adam Clarke, *Memoirs of the Wesley Family*

Her father was not moved. Susanna again pleaded with him. "Samuel, can you not find it in your heart to forgive her? I am sure she is truly repentant."

"If she thinks to persuade me her penitence is more than feigned, she is going the wrong way to work. I decline to be a party to her matrimonial fortunes and I shall write to tell her so."

He stamped off and Susanna had no doubt he would do so. Why was her husband so stubborn? And Hetty was as bad. If she had not flown in the face of convention and refused to listen to her father, there would not now be trouble between them. Susanna sighed as she returned to her work. She would have liked to visit her wayward child but Samuel would refuse to let her go and she was too tired to keep arguing with him.

Matthew Wesley came to his niece's aid and gave the couple five hundred pounds which enabled them to move to London where William was able to start his plumbing business again. Samuel was never reconciled to his erring daughter.

CHAPTER TEN

Exiled To Wroot

Wroot was not a healthy place to live. It was damp all the year and when the rains came, it became flooded and impassable by road. Susanna took to her bed and her health deteriorated but she maintained her customary calm. Emilia too became ill with malaria. She had never been happy at Wroot and eventually she told her mother she wished to return to Lincoln to seek employment.

"I am never well, here, Mama, and my life is drifting away. I wish you could come with me."

"You know that is not possible, my child. I must stay with your father." She misquoted from the Book of Ruth. "Where he lives, I will live and where he dies will I die and there will I be buried."

Emilia sighed. Her father had become even more irascible of late and she would be glad to be free of him for a while but she would be sad to leave her mother. Her good intentions to stay had evaporated and she wanted to escape from her cage.

"I am sorry to leave you, Mama, but I believe I must. I think there is employment to be had and I am a good teacher. I had the best training," she ended, smiling at her mother.

Susanna gave a weak smile. "God go with you, my dear."

Emilia found employment in a boarding school run by a Mrs Taylor in Lincoln. It was not long before this lady realised the worth of her new employee and soon Emilia was running the school but being paid a meagre salary. Kezzy, her youngest sister, later also became a pupil-teacher at the same school.

Losing her daughters was a blow but early in 1726 came news that delighted both Susanna and her husband and made them forget for a while all their trials and tribulations. On March 17th John was elected as a Fellow of Lincoln College, Oxford. It had been financially difficult for the Wesleys to support John at Oxford but now all their sacrifices were shown to be worthwhile. As well as the honour of the Fellowship, John would be able to live rent-free in the college and would also be given an annual stipend.

"He will be able to help Charles when he goes to Christ Church in September," reflected the practical Susanna. "But first he has to pay £12 for the honour; Samuel, we do not have the money."

"Nothing must stand in his way." Samuel refused to be depressed. "I will write to my good friend, Dr Morley at Oxford. I am sure he will advance me the money." His plea was successful and Samuel wrote to his son.

Dear Mr Fellow-Elect of Lincoln,

I have done more than I could for you. On your waiting on Dr Morley with this he will pay you £12. You are inexpressibly obliged to that generous man. We are all as well as can be expected.

Your loving father,

Samuel Wesley[43]

---

43   Sir Arthur Quiller-Couch, *Hetty Wesley*

Debt was an ever present visitor in the Wesley household and the £12 added yet another burden and Samuel wrote again to his son. The euphoria had gone and his depression at his financial state was clear although his pride was evident in his last sentence.

> Dear son John,
>
> The last £12 pinched me so hard that I am forced to beg time of your brother Sam till after harvest to pay him the £10 that you say he lent you. Nor shall I have so much as that to keep my family till after harvest; and I do not expect that I shall be able to do anything for Charles when he goes to the University. What will be my own fate before the summer is over God only knows. Wherever I am, my Jack is Fellow of Lincoln.
>
> All at present from your loving father,
>
> Samuel Wesley.[44]

His father's decline in health upset John and, to his mother's delight, he set out for Wroot where he stayed for several months to help his father, sometimes preaching twice on Sundays either at Wroot or Epworth. Samuel also persuaded him to help with his work on Job which, since his illness and his inability to write easily had been progressing very slowly.

The summer of 1727 had more rain than anyone could remember. The floods came almost to the door of the Parsonage and Samuel became twisted with rheumatism as a result of his journeys to Epworth. He complained that his breeches became heavy with water not only from the rain but also from the wash from the small boat in which he had to travel.

---

44   ibid.

John returned to Oxford to resume his studies on 21st September 1727 and took his Master's Degree on February 14th 1728. To Susanna's delight and Samuel's relief he returned to Wroot to help his ailing father who was now sixty-five. He stayed until July 1728 when he returned to Oxford.

Soon after he left, Samuel sustained a nasty fall from his horse. He later described the incident to John in a letter. 'My old nag fell with me, trailed me by my foot in the stirrups about six yards, trod on my other foot, yet never hurt me.'[45]

On this occasion he was alone but when, three weeks later, a more serious accident occurred, fortunately, Johnny Whitelamb was with him. Johnny had continued to work with Samuel but found his mater's temper trying at times. He was glad to escape from the Rector's study and help Molly to grow vegetables in the kitchen garden which she had extended with his help. She also bred poultry and helped to eke out the family's meagre income by selling surplus vegetables and eggs at Epworth market. She and John were becoming very friendly although he was fourteen years younger than she was.

One late August morning in 1728 the Rector came into the study where John was working alone. "John, I should like you to walk with me to Froddingham where I have to transact some business."

Johnny looked up, surprised. "But surely, Sir, after your recent fall you would find it difficult to walk so far."

"I shall ride Bounce and you will walk beside me. Then you shall rescue me should I fall," the Rector announced with a rare touch of humour.

---

45   Arnold A. Dallimore, *Susanna Wesley.*

"Very well, Sir, but could I not be your messenger?"

"No, Johnny. I must go myself."

Susanna was in the yard as Bounce was led out. She stared at her husband. "You are surely not going to ride, Samuel. You are not fit."

"I have to go to Froddingham."

"But surely Johnny can go for you."

"No." The Rector's lips tightened and he flicked the reins on the mare's flank and she set off at a walking pace.

Susanna looked after him with pity. "Take care of him, Johnny."

"I will, ma'am." He walked swiftly off, catching up with the ambling mare with no difficulty.

It was a grey blustery morning and the wind left no breath for talking. Although the floods had subsided, the River Trent which they had to cross at Althorpe was threatening to overflow its banks. Johnny gazed anxiously at the water as they waited for the boat which would take them across to the other side. He was further concerned to discover that the usual ferryman was not on duty and his son had co-opted his younger brother, scarcely more than a child to help him. This did not give Johnny confidence.

"Perhaps we should not go," he suggested to Samuel, eyeing the rocking boat with trepidation.

But Samuel was already coaxing Bounce on board. He stood, holding her bridle, in the middle of the boat. Johnny climbed in and sat facing the rowers as the boat was pushed off from the shore. The water was becoming rougher and half way across, the young boy suddenly panicked and dropped his oar. The boat jerked and turned. Suddenly there was a grinding crash and water poured over them. The mare drifted away while Johnny was flung on top of Samuel. Grasping the Rector's collar with one hand, he found a piece of wreckage anchored in the water and grasped it.

He was just beginning to give up hope of being rescued when he heard shouting. Rough hands laid hold of him and the two half drowned men were hauled to safety on board a collier.[46] The young oarsman who had caused the disaster, had already clambered on to the deck and was shivering with fear and cold. His brother was swimming strongly to safety.

Samuel coughed and tried to sit up. "The mare," he croaked. "Where is she?"

One of their rescuers pointed. "She'll reach the shore before you will."

As they watched, the mare and the boy struggled ashore and collapsed on the bank. Samuel forced himself to his knees and to the embarrassment of the assembled company, announced, "We must give thanks to Almighty God for his mercy in rescuing us."

Sheepishly the sailors removed their caps and they and the erstwhile oarsman knelt on the wet deck while Samuel delivered a lengthy prayer of thanksgiving. Sneaking a glance at the embarrassed men, Johnny wondered irreverently whether the sailors, on board the boat on which Paul had been shipwrecked, had reacted in the same way when the Apostle had prayed.

When Samuel had finished, the sailors slid a small boat into the water and the dripping Johnny and Samuel were helped into it and ferried to the shore. Bounce, shivering and caked in mud awaited them. Johnny helped his master to remount and, limping they retraced their steps to the Parsonage where Johnny led the mare to the stable and tried to clean her up. Samuel was met at the door by a shocked Susanna.

"Oh, Samuel, I warned you not to go."

---

46   A coal boat

"I am all right, Sukey," coughed Samuel.

She fussed around him. "Go and change into dry clothes and I will make you some hot broth."

He limped off and she bustled into the kitchen where he rejoined her a little later.

"You should not do so much, Samuel," she scolded. "You must not go out when the weather is so bad."

"Don't fuss, Sukey. I am all right." He sipped the hot liquid, slopping a little as his hands were shaking.

She watched him anxiously. When he had finished the broth, she said gently, "What happened?"

"Johnny saved my life today."

"Oh!" Susanna's hand flew to her mouth as Samuel recounted what had happened.

"Thank God Johnny was with you," was all she could say when he had finished.

"We all thanked him, my dear. And now I must acknowledge my debt to Whitelamb. For some time now it has been in my mind to send him to Oxford. What think you, Sukey?"

"Oh, yes. He deserves it thoroughly and he will do you credit. But Molly will be sad to see him go."

"He will return and perhaps may be of even more use to us."

"That is true."

"I will write to Jack. I am sure he will take Johnny for his pupil and I must hammer some Greek into him before he goes. Now I will send for him to my study and inform him of my decision."

Johnny was overwhelmed when he heard of his good fortune. To go to Oxford had for long been a dream of his but he had not thought it would ever come true. At supper that night the talk was all of the rescue and of Johnny's future.

Molly smiled across the table at him. "I think Johnny will be as great a man as Jack in time. I will miss your help in the garden, Johnny."

"I will help you when I return."

"Johnny deserves his good fortune. He has done so much for all of us over the years." Susanna smiled at the young man. "May God go with you, Son."

Johnny had trouble to hold back the tears at the salutation. She had never called him that before but from the time Samuel had taken him in, she had treated him as a son. He would miss her but he would return. He was sure of it. This was his home.

He went up to Oxford in September. Susanna and Molly both missed the young man who had always been so willing to help them with tasks around the house and land. On 22nd September 1728, John Wesley was ordained priest by Dr Potter, the same Bishop who had ordained him deacon three years previously.

After his ordination he returned to Wroot as Samuel's curate while Johnny Whitelamb remained at Oxford. John felt he owed something to Samuel who had sacrificed so much in order to enable his son to go to Oxford. Although the congregation at Wroot was small and living conditions poor, John enjoyed the time and he might have remained there had not the Rector of Lincoln College demanded his return to Oxford to fulfil his obligations as a Fellow of the College. He left Wroot and returned to Oxford on 22nd November 1729.

In 1731 the Wesleys moved back to the Epworth Rectory. Susanna was relieved. The dampness of Wroot had been detrimental to her health and she had not been well for some time. Molly was disappointed that the kitchen garden she had tended with such care would no longer provide produce to sell but she planned to reproduce her work at Epworth.

The Ellisons had moved out and had found a property a few miles away where Richard could farm.

Soon after they moved Samuel had another accident. It was Friday 4th June. Had it not been for the quick-thinking of the maid, Susanna too might have been injured. They were travelling in the wagon to visit a neighbour. Samuel was sitting in a chair at one end of the vehicle while Susanna sat at the other with Patty between them. The maid was sitting behind her mistress.

Suddenly, going down a small hill, the horses decided to gallop and Susanna watched in horror as her husband and his chair flew off the wagon and fell heavily on the ground.

The maid, gripping Susanna's chair to prevent it going the same way, screamed, "William, stop the horses. My master is killed!"

"Oh no!" gasped Susanna as the wagon jolted and almost threw her as William brought the horses under control. The man leapt out of his seat and ran towards his master but two neighbours reached him first. He had obviously hit his head on the ground and his face was black.

"He's not breathing," wailed Patty.

"He's all right, Ma'am," said one of the men, holding the Rector's head. "See he's breathing again now."

"Thank God," moaned Susanna kneeling by her husband. "Patty, get the ale we brought with us. Hurry." She turned back to her husband. "How do you do, husband?"

Samuel sat up. His hat had fallen off and his wig was awry. He looked wildly at her. "I am well, woman. Why do you ask?" he demanded irritably.

"You fell from the wagon, Samuel, and hit your head."

"I know nothing of any fall. I am as well as ever I was in my life."

"Here is the ale, Mama." Patty handed it to her mother.

"Take a little, Samuel. It will help the shock." She held the flask to her husband's lips and he spluttered. "Your poor head is much bruised. Let me bind it for you and then we will go home."

Having treated her husband as well as she could, she helped him back to the wagon. "William, lead the horses softly home. Your master must not be shaken."

"Yes, Ma'am."

Susanna held her husband's head between her hands and they drove back to the Rectory where, in spite of his objections, Susanna put Samuel to bed and sent for the physician, Mr Harper, who took some blood from him. Samuel began to feel pain in other parts of his body and the next day Mr Harper again visited to bind his head and give him something to ease the pain in his side.

On the Sunday, Susanna tried unsuccessfully to persuade her husband to stay in bed.

"I have to take the services, Sukey. I cannot leave my flock without a shepherd."

"I am sure they would understand. Mr Hoole from Haxey might perhaps take one of the services."

"No, Sukey. I must do it."

Susanna sighed. Why was her husband so stubborn? He took two services that day and not surprisingly was very ill on the following Monday. For once he made no objection to staying in bed and he slept almost all the day. The next day he had an attack of gout.

"I am afraid the wagon may have gone over him although we did not realise it at the time," Susanna told Mr Harper.

"No, my dear Mrs Wesley you need not trouble yourself on that account. I think it may have gone over his gown sleeve only. The nails took a little skin off his knuckles but he has sustained no further hurt. He will be well soon, if only he will rest." [47]

"It is hard to make him do so," sighed Susanna. She was worried about him. He was now nearly sixty-nine and was becoming frailer. Life became no easier for Susanna but an unexpected visitor soon after the accident proved very welcome to them both. Samuel's brother, Matthew, who was now seventy-seven and had retired from his work, decided at last to make the long journey to Epworth. Although he was not short of money and had travelled widely in Europe, he had never visited his poverty stricken brother although he had always welcomed members of the Wesley family to his luxurious home in London.

He did not let the family know he was coming and travelled under an assumed name from London to Gainsborough which he reached on a Thursday in July. Once there, he sent his servant to ask the way to Epworth. Few people visited this isolated area and his questions provoked curiosity. Delighted to be the centre of attention, the man announced that his master was going to see his brother who was the minister at Epworth. Word spread to Epworth that an important visitor was on his way.

Molly, shopping in the market, heard the news and hurried home. Hurriedly depositing her purchases on the kitchen table, she exclaimed, "Mama, Uncle Wesley is coming to visit us."

Susanna looked up, startled, from the table where she was preparing the vegetables for dinner. "Your Uncle Wesley, here?"

"His man was enquiring directions in Gainsborough. Tom Cobb heard him and hurried back to spread the news.

---

47   The words used are taken from Samuel's letter to his son John dated July 12th 1731: in G.J. Stevenson, *Memorials of the Wesley Family.*

He is at Gainsborough under a feigned name. I think he wished to surprise us."

"How strange of him," mused Susanna. "Of course he must come here to stay." She turned to the man servant. "John Brown, go at once to John Dawson's Inn and wait there. When Mr Wesley comes, invite him to our house."

"Yes, Mrs Wesley." The man hurried off and Susanna looked at her daughter. "We must prepare for our visitor. Go to your father's study and tell him the news."

It was not long before there was a bustle outside and John Brown escorted Matthew Wesley into the kitchen and he looked around him with bewilderment. Susanna saw that he was shocked at the bareness of the room. However, he was perfectly civil during the time he spent with them and did not appear to be critical of the way they lived.

Susanna knew he spoke quite freely to Patty and Molly. Kezzy, now fifteen, had joined Emilia at Mrs Taylor's school in Lincoln, so there were only the two girls left at home. Although perfectly polite, Susanna was sure her brother-in-law was critical of her husband for not providing adequately for his family. She wrote later to her son John that his uncle had been 'strangely scandalised at the poverty of our furniture and much more at the meanness of the children's habit.' [48]

Hoping he would not think she was about to beg from him, Susanna decided she should explain why they were not able to live in the luxurious style to which he was accustomed in London.

"You must wonder at our poor living conditions, brother," she remarked one morning before Samuel had put

---

48   Sir Arthur Quiller-Couch, *Hetty Wesle*

in an appearance. Before he could reply, she continued. "You must know that we have had great losses. Twice the Rectory has been on fire and the second time it burnt down completely and we lost everything." Her voice broke as she remembered her father's precious books and papers.

"It must have been a great sadness, sister," said Matthew gently.

Susanna recovered herself. "Indeed it was but at least God was gracious to us and saved our children — even Jackie who was so near death. Truly he was a brand plucked from the burning." Matthew nodded looking thoughtful. At last he said, "Sister, I have already endeavoured to make one of your children easy while she lives and if you choose to trust Patty with me, I will endeavour to make her so too." [49]

"That is a most generous offer, brother. Will you speak with my husband on the matter?"

"I would rather leave that to you. You will know how to approach him."

"Very well."

"I will leave with Patty on Sunday. We will stop at Lincoln to visit Emilia and Kezziah. I have in mind to invite them to dine with me at the Angel on Sunday night — and perhaps Mrs Taylor too, if she will."

"That is most kind. The girls will be pleased to see you."

Patty was thrilled to be invited to stay with her uncle and she made her home with him for several years. Matthew had been charming all the time he had been a visitor in the Epworth Rectory. Although Kezzy was not living at home at the time, she was shocked that her sister should go to

---

49   Stevenson, *Memorials of the Wesley Family*

London. Perhaps she also regretted that she had not been invited too. She wrote to John from Lincoln:

> Indeed sister Pat's going to London shocked me a little, because it was unexpected; and perhaps may have been the cause of my ill health for the last fortnight. It would not have had so great an effect upon my mind if I had known it before.

At the end of the letter was a heartfelt plea:

> Pray, desire sister Pat to write by you. I have not heard from her since she went. You must not measure the length of your next letter by mine; I am ill, and can't write any more.

Kezzy had never enjoyed the best of health but she was spared the unhappiness caused in the Epworth household by a letter from Matthew Wesley. Samuel was greatly disturbed by it and both he and Susanna felt that it was unjust. His brother wrote that the conditions in which the Rector's family lived had disgusted him and he was convinced it was due to his brother's poor financial management. He was concerned that after Samuel's death, his family would be left destitute. He wrote:

> You have numerous offspring; you have had a long time a plentiful estate, great and generous benefactions, and made no provision for those of your own house, who can have nothing in view at your exit but distress. This, I think, a black account, let the case be folly, or vanity, or ungovernable appetites.
>
> I hope Providence has restored you again to give you time to settle this balance, which shocks me to think of.[50]

Although Samuel was not adept at managing his financial affairs, he felt the letter to be grossly unjust as his salary was

---

50   Stevenson, *Memorials of the Wesley Family*

considerably less than that of his brother and in spite of his financial problems he had managed, as he told his brother, to give his sons 'the best education England could afford.' He agreed he had numerous offspring but, he wrote, he had no reason to be ashamed of any of them — apart from Hetty. He was sure, he told his brother, that God would look after his family after his death. He then detailed the money he had received and his expenditure, stressing the two fires that had damaged the Rectory. He concluded,

> There are many gentlemen's families in England who ...
> would be glad to change the best of theirs ... for almost
> the worst of [mine]. [51]

His brother's reproof, his accident and the increasing frailty, which made administering two parishes difficult, caused Samuel to think about the future. He started to worry about how his wife would manage after his death. However he did nothing practical for some time.

Emilia at this time was becoming increasingly dissatisfied with her life in Lincoln. Mrs Taylor expected too much of her and she was poorly paid. In 1732 she decided to start her own school at Gainsborough. She had the support of her brothers, Sammy and John and no doubt they helped her financially. Like her mother, she was a good teacher and her school was successful.

In 1733 Samuel eventually made a decision about the future. He wrote to Sammy asking him to apply for the living at Epworth.

> Dear Sammy
> For several reasons, I have earnestly desired ... that you
> might succeed me at Epworth ... As for your aged and
> infirm mother, as soon as I drop, she must turn out,

---

51   Ibid

unless you succeed me; which if you do, and she survives me, I know you will then immediately continue her there, where your wife and you will nourish her, till we meet in heaven. [52]

To his father's distress, Sammy refused the offer and the following year the same offer was made to John who also declined it to Susanna's disappointment. She longed to have her favourite son near her again.

---

52   Stevenson, *Memorials of the Wesley Family*

CHAPTER ELEVEN

Susanna Mourns For Samuel

Samuel was becoming weaker. Johnny Whitelamb had now followed in his benefactor's footsteps and been ordained. *He* had no hesitation in accepting Samuel's offer to become his curate. He had not forgotten Molly. Crippled though she was, she had a sweetness of character and he had frequently thought of her during his time at Oxford although he had had a dalliance with a Miss Betty while there. Soon after his return to Epworth he proposed to her and she accepted him. Samuel was delighted but Susanna had heard about Johnny's affair and, remembering the trials of her other daughters, was not so happy. However, on this occasion, she did not voice her objections. Johnny had been like a son to them and she could see how happy Molly was.

Soon after they were married, Samuel said to his wife, "If the Lord Chancellor agrees, I shall resign the living of Wroot to John."

Susanna, who had recovered her affection for Johnny, smiled. "That is an excellent idea. Molly and Johnny love Wroot and it will be a good start for them." Samuel accordingly wrote to the Lord Chancellor.[54]

My Lord,

The small Rectory of Wroot, in the diocese and County of Lincoln, adjoining to the Isle of Axholme, is in the gift of the Lord Chancellor, and more than seven years since was conferred on Samuel Wesley, Rector of Epworth … This living, by your Lordship's permission and favour, I would gladly resign to one Mr John Whitelamb, born in the neighbourhood of Wroot, as his father and grandfather lived in it, when I took him from among the scholars of a Charity School…, brought him to my house and educated him there, where he was my amanuensis[55] for four years … After this, I sent him to Oxford, to my son John Wesley, Fellow of Lincoln College, under whom he made such proficiency, that he was the last summer admitted by the Bishop of Oxford into Deacon's Orders, and placed my curate in Epworth.

… I gave consent to his marrying one of my seven daughters and they are married accordingly; and though I can spare little more with her, yet I would gladly give them a little glebe land at Wroot … they love the place, though I can get nobody else to reside on it.

If I do not flatter myself, he is indeed a valuable person; of uncommon brightness, learning piety, and indefatigable industry; always loyal to the King, zealous for the Church, and friendly to the Dissenting Brethren; and for the truth of this character I will be answerable to God and man. If, therefore, your Lordship will grant me the favour to let me resign the Living unto him, and please to confer it on him, I shall always remain,

---

54   Stevenson, *Memorials of the Wesley Family*
55   One who copies Samuel's work for him.

Your Lordship's most bounden, most grateful, and most obedient servant

Samuel Wesley

The Lord Chancellor agreed to Samuel's request and in February 1734 with an income increased to seventy pounds a year, Johnny Whitelamb and his newly pregnant wife took possession of the small rectory at Wroot.

Their happiness was short lived. In October Molly gave birth but the baby died soon afterwards. Poor, frail Molly soon followed her child and she died in her distraught husband's arms at the end of 1734. Her brother, John, preached at the funeral service at Wroot; Samuel Junior wrote a eulogy and Hetty penned an epitaph for her sister; the latter never appeared on Mary's tombstone but was published in *The Gentleman's Magazine* in 1736.

Meanwhile in London Patty had met a young clergyman, Westley Hall, who had been at Oxford with her brothers. They became secretly engaged. Even John did not know of this when he invited the young man to accompany him to Epworth. Kezzy was also staying at the Rectory at the time and she and Westley became very friendly.

Concerned though she was about her husband, Susanna was aware that her daughter had started to bloom. Her ailments had disappeared and she seemed healthier than she had done for weeks. Her mother was sure her new radiance was connected with their visitor.

"He seems a very pleasant young man," she told her son. "Do you think he is attracted to Kezzy?"

"He spends a great deal of time with her. I know she likes him."

"I should be glad if she could be settled. She is such a dear child."

John agreed. He was very fond of Kezzy who did not share the beauty of her sisters. Neither was she as intelligent but she was desperate to acquire knowledge and John wrote to her frequently. He was glad she was happy and hoped that Westley Hall's intentions were honourable. Neither he nor his mother were aware of Westley's engagement to Patty.

Johnny Whitelamb was still grieving ceaselessly for his lost wife. A neighbour had taken pity on him and came to the Rectory each day to prepare food for him. But when the Church bell summoned the parishioners to church on Sunday, he sat in his study staring unseeingly at an open book. He had prepared no sermon. He was not even aware it was the Lord's Day. It was here John Wesley found him after he had walked over from Epworth. Unable to rouse him to his duties, John took his place and preached at Wroot on that Sunday. After the service, he returned to the Rectory at Wroot.

"You cannot sit here grieving day after day," he told the widower. "Surely sister Molly would not have wished that. My father is ill and wishes to complete his work on the 'Dissertations on the Book of Job'. He would be glad to employ you again as his amanuensis. Will you come when he sends for you?"

Johnny sighed. "I will come."

"Do you think he will do so?" Susanna asked her son when she heard of his visit.

"I think he will. He cannot grieve alone. It will be good for him to come."

Susanna nodded. She, too, was grieving deeply for her gentle daughter and she was concerned about her husband.

"He is becoming weaker every day," she told John sadly. "I fear he will not be with us much longer."

"Have faith, Mother. God will take him in his own time and he will surely care for you."

"I know it. I have felt the Holy Spirit very close to me in these last days."

John and Westley Hall returned to Oxford and, perhaps conscience-stricken by his flirtation with Kezzy while engaged to her sister, Westley returned to Patty. Early in 1735 they were married in London with the blessing of Matthew Wesley. Kezzy was heartbroken and Susanna could do nothing to comfort her.

"I thought he loved *me*, " she sobbed.

"I thought so, too," said her mother gently. "But apparently he was secretly engaged to Patty when he came down here."

"How could he behave like that?" wailed Kezzy.

"I do not know my dear, but you are better without him. I only hope Patty will not live to regret her marriage."

"I never liked the man from the first time I saw him," growled her husband.

They were right to be apprehensive. Their daughter had married a philanderer and Patty led a life of misery. Of the ten children she bore him, only one survived and even this boy died of smallpox at the early age of fourteen. For a while Patty was unaware of her husband's unfaithfulness but when one of her servants went into labour and she was told the child was his, Hall left her. Showing great forbearance, she forgave him and persuaded him to return but he did not mend his ways.

Soon after Patty's marriage, Johnny Whitelamb walked over to Epworth to help Samuel with his masterpiece on Job. The work proceeded slowly.

"He is in a very bad state of health," Susanna said sadly to Johnny Whitelamb. "He sleeps little and eats less. I fear he has but a short time to live."

"He performs Divine Service on the Lord's Day with much difficulty," Johnny agreed. "But he seems not to have any apprehension of his approaching exit."

Susanna nodded. "Everybody observes his decay but himself. He insists on going to London to promote his book. But I shall send John Brown to escort him home."

That was Samuel's last trip to London. As 1735 moved into the Spring, it was obvious to Susanna that her husband would not last much longer. Only Kezzy was still at home with her.

"Your father is not long for this world," she told her daughter. "I must send for your brothers and Emilia must return from Gainsborough."

On 25th April 1735 Susanna, Emilia, Sukey, John and Charles were gathered round Samuel's bed. The end was near.

John leant over his father. "Sir, are you in much pain?"

The faintest of whispers came back. "God chastens all my bones with strong pain but I thank him for it. I love him for all."

"You are near Heaven, father," murmured John.

"Yes, son, I am." He struggled to say something else and they leant closer to hear. "Think of Heaven. Talk of Heaven. Time is lost when we are not thinking of Heaven. Nothing is too much to suffer for Heaven. The weaker I am in body, the more support I feel from God. Now, children, I desire that I may once more eat the bread and drink the cup of blessing with you before I die."

John moved away from the bed and carried the elements to his father. Those around his bed joined him in the sacred act. Afterwards Samuel sank back on his pillow smiling faintly. The pain had disappeared from his face and he looked peaceful. Emilia, who had been holding back her tears with difficulty, suddenly sobbed quietly and her father's eyes turned to her.

"Do not be concerned at my death, daughter," he said gently. "Remember that the inward witness is the strongest proof of Christianity. I know that after my death, God will begin to manifest himself to my family in a marvellous way." He paused and then added the prophecy that within a decade was to be fulfilled, surpassing anything he could have imagined. *"The Christian faith will surely revive in this Kingdom. You will see it, though I shall not."*

As the daylight faded, John said aloud the commendatory prayer. As it ended, Samuel's life ebbed away. He was seventy-two. John gently closed his father's eyes and Emilia sobbed again.

"He looks so peaceful," she whispered. "Has he really gone?"

"He's free from pain now in the presence of his God," said Charles gently.

Susanna drew a long shuddering breath and her children looked anxiously at her. She had found it so hard to watch her beloved husband dying and had frequently collapsed in the sick room. But now she found an inner strength that surprised her family.

She smiled at them. "I am glad that he had so easy a death and I know God has strengthened me to bear it." [56]

Samuel had hoped to die free from debt but that was not to be. The news of his death travelled fast and to Susanna's horror, her husband was hardly cold when she heard a commotion in the fields outside. Looking out of the window,

---

56   The account of Samuel's death is adapted from *The Life and Times of Samuel Wesley* by Luke Tyerman

she saw a woman brandishing a stick and herding Samuel's cattle through the open gate. She gasped and John joined her at the window.

"We must stop her. What is she doing?" cried Susanna.

John's eyes were sharper. "I fear Father's creditors are already baying for their dues. It is Mrs Knight from Low Mellwood, Mother."

"But ... " Susanna, still shocked from her husband's death, followed her son downstairs and out into the fields. He was right. Mrs Knight turned back and came to face them.

Brandishing her stick, she growled, "These cattle are mine by right. Your father owed me fifteen pounds. He said he would pay me, but he never did. The cattle will do instead."

Susanna turned away, tears blinding her. Was her husband not even to die in peace? John followed his mother back to the house. There was nothing he could do although the cattle were worth more than fifteen pounds.

"You must not worry, Mother," he said gently. "I will pay off the debts and take care of you."

She gazed at him through her tears. "I know you will, my son."

Samuel was buried quietly in the churchyard of Epworth, the parish he had served for so many years. His son, Sammy, completed his work on Job and six months after his death John presented the bound copy to Queen Caroline to whom his father had dedicated it.

The Queen received it graciously. "It is very prettily bound," she said kindly, laying it down without a second glance. John bowed and left the presence. How sad that his father's life's work should be reduced to a mere comment on its binding.

Susanna was broken-hearted at her husband's death. She had had her differences with him but she had loved him deeply and although he had not always shown it, she knew he had cared for her. John settled the debts that had hung over his mother all her married life. They amounted to over an hundred pounds and when all their goods were sold, there was little left over for Susanna. The sideboard that had stood in the Rectory during all the time they had lived there was sold to the Red Lion Inn in the village where John often stayed when he returned to Epworth. [53] Samuel's chair Susanna donated to the Church he had served so faithfully.

"You must come to Gainsborough to live with me, Mama," Emilia said when everything was settled. "You will be able to rest a little. You have worked so hard. Now is the time to be easy."

Susanna allowed herself to be guided. Now that Samuel was gone, she had lost the motivation that had kept her going. Her faith was still strong and she knew Samuel was now safe in the arms of his Lord and free from pain. But she had little interest in her future. She would do her duty by her remaining children if they needed her, but she felt her life's work was over. She was waiting to join her husband.

However God had other plans for her. She still had a great work to do in her declining years.

---

[53] It has now been returned to the Rectory and stands in the entrance hall.

CHAPTER TWELVE

The Widow Makes Her Mark

The wagon stood waiting. Sammy, Kezzy and Emilia stood beside the open door waiting for Susanna. Sammy, who was now Headmaster of Blundells School in Tiverton, Devon, had not, to his mother's sorrow, been able to reach Epworth before his father died. But he had come as soon as he could and helped to make his mother's last days in the Rectory as stress free as he could. Kezzy, the only daughter still living at home, would return with him to Tiverton to live.

Emilia looked up impatiently. "Come, Mama. The wagon waits for us." Susanna looked down from the top of the stairs. Her eyes were sad. "You must be patient, my dear. I am leaving the home I have lived in for more than half of my life."

"I am sorry, Mama. I will wait for you."

"She will find it hard. You must be gentle with her," Sammy rebuked his sister.

"I know. I am hoping she will help in the school. She has always been so busy. I cannot imagine her being idle."

"She is an excellent teacher," thoughtfully remarked Kezzy.

Upstairs, Susanna went into her husband's study and stood at the window gazing out at the windmill for the last time. She turned to open the cupboard door. One of Samuel's wigs still hung on its hook. Tears pricked her eyes as she hurriedly closed the door and stumbled from the room. Her last visit was to the bedroom she had shared with Samuel.

She looked around. In this room she had borne twelve of her nineteen children. Her gaze fell on the chair she had used for her meditations. There was a drawer to hold her large Bible and a flap that could be pulled down on which she had rested her Bible as she knelt in front of it. There was no Bible there now. It was packed in her trunk but she kneeled down as she had done so many times before.

Shutting her eyes, she prayed softly, "Oh Loving Heavenly Father God, I ask thy mercies on me now as I leave this place. Bless all those who live here in the future."

Easing herself carefully to her feet, she gave a last look round and then closed the door behind her. Slowly she walked down the stairs and out of the house she was never to see again. She did not look back as the wagon drove her away from Epworth and to the start of a new life.

Her daughters were right about her teaching. She was delighted to help Emilia in the school and her pupils loved her. Emilia's mind, however, was not completely on her work. She had fallen in love again. This time her swain was Robert Harper; he came from Epworth and had been known to the Wesley family for some years. He practised as an apothecary, but without being licensed.

"He has asked me to marry him, Mama," Emilia told her mother one evening. Her cheeks were flushed. Susanna waited. "I have agreed to do so. We would like the marriage to take place soon. Do you think Jacky will perform the ceremony."

"I'm sure he will. I am glad for you, my child. I hope you will be happy." Whatever reservations Susanna had, she kept them to herself. She was aware, as her daughter must also be, that Robert Harper was not a financial success. She hoped the marriage would last.

"You will still stay with us," Emilia said anxiously.

"If I shall not be intruding."

"Of course not. We would be very unhappy if you left."

"Thank you, my dear."

Emilia and Robert were married towards the end of 1735. She was forty three. She had had other suitors but had not been married before. She had once been desperately in love with Robert Leybourne, a fellow student of John's at Oxford. She had met him when staying with her uncle Matthew in London and the romance had lasted three years. Emilia was sure they would get married but her eldest brother, Sammy, disagreed and managed to prevent the wedding. Although heartbroken at the time, Emilia later realised that Leybourne would not have made her happy and had not even been in love with her. She hoped this other Robert would make a better husband.

John performed the ceremony. He also had a decision to make and he needed to consult his mother about it. He was not happy about this but others had prevailed upon him to seek his mother's advice.

One evening they sat facing each other in Emilia's small sitting room. Susanna was delighted to see her favourite son again but she knew something was worrying him.

"What is it, my son? I know you are anxious. Can you not tell me?"

He sighed. "Mama, you remember the colony that General Oglethorpe established in Georgia in America two years ago."

Susanna thought for a moment. "It is a refuge for English clergymen in jail for debt. Yes I remember. Your father was very interested in it and so, I believe, is your eldest brother."

John nodded. "They sent a paten and chalice for administering the Sacrament in the new colony."

There was a pause and Susanna looked directly at her son. "You wish to ask me something, Jacky?"

"General Oglethorpe has organised a second group of immigrants who wish to practise their faith in Georgia. They sail for America soon."

"And you wish to go with them," stated Susanna calmly.

Her son looked startled. "They have asked me to go as their chaplain but I refused—because I did not wish to leave you. But I have been prevailed upon to reconsider and to seek your advice in the matter."

Susanna smiled. "If I had twenty sons, I should rejoice that they were all so profitably employed even though I might never see them more."

"Oh, Mama."

"Go, my son, with my blessing."

"There is something else. Charles, too, has been asked to go — as Secretary to General Oglethorpe. He also asks for your blessing."

"He has it. May God bless you both."

John and Charles left England on 14th October 1735 and it was some time before Susanna saw either of them again. She stayed with Emilia until the September of the following year when she went to live in Tiverton with Sammy and his family. Also living there were Mrs Berry, Samuel's mother-in-law and Kezzy. But Kezzy was soon to leave.

"I have had a letter from Patty, Mama," she told her mother excitedly. "She suggests I go and live with them in London."

Susanna looked startled. "My dear, is that wise after the way Mr Hall treated you?"

"That is forgotten. He chose to marry Patty. I would like to go, Mama."

"It is your choice, Kezzy, but you must think carefully about it."

Whether her youngest daughter took her advice or not, she accepted the invitation and lived happily with the Halls for several years.

Susanna was now sixty-seven and she was becoming frailer and was often confined to her bed. But her faith was as strong as ever it had been and she remained cheerful. When Charles returned from Georgia in December 1736, she was delighted to see him although sorry to hear the trip had not been a success.

"It was not as we expected, Mama." Charles was discouraged and Susanna tried to cheer him.

"What of your brother?"

"He remains but, I think, not for much longer."

When John returned, equally discouraged, the following year, Susanna was living with the Halls. Both brothers contemplated returning to Georgia at some time but Susanna vehemently dissuaded them.

"You are far better suited to be clergymen in England, my sons," she told them. How right she was although she could not have foreseen the dramatic events of the following years.

After her husband's death, Susanna did more travelling than she had done all the years she had been married to Samuel. When the Halls moved to Fisherton near Salisbury, Susanna went with them. Her health had improved and she enjoyed the time with her daughter and son-in-law who were both very kind to her. It was not until later that Westley Hall reverted to his true colours, deserting his wife and fleeing to the West Indies with his current mistress.

In May 1738 occurred the event that was to have such a far reaching effect on this country. The events of Wednesday 24th May were recorded in John Wesley's diary.

> In the evening I went very unwillingly to a society in Aldersgate Street, where one was reading Luther's preface to the *Epistle to the Romans.* About a quarter before nine, while he was describing the change which God works in the heart through faith in Christ, I felt my heart strangely warmed. I felt I did trust in Christ, Christ alone for salvation; and an assurance was given me that he had taken away *my* sins, even *mine* and saved *me* from the law of sin and death. [57]

His brother, Charles, had undergone a similar conversion three days previously. Both brothers were now convinced that sins could only be forgiven if one accepted that Christ had died to save sinners. Full of their new found faith, the brothers wrote to their mother and John travelled round the country preaching and converting hundreds of the people who turned out to hear him.

Susanna was bewildered by what had happened to her sons. She wrote to Charles:

> I think you are fallen into an odd way of thinking. You say that till within a few months, you had no spiritual life, nor any justifying faith.
>
> Now this is as if a man should affirm he was not alive in his infancy, because when an infant, he did not know he was alive. All then that I gather from your letter is that, till a little while ago you were not so well satisfied of your being a Christian as you are now. I heartily rejoice that

---

[57] The Journal of John Wesley, May 24, 1738

you have now attained to a strong and lively hope in God's mercy through Christ. Not that I can think that you were totally without saving faith before: but it is one thing to have faith, and another thing to be sensible we have it.[58]

Their eldest brother disapproved strongly of his brothers' activities which he felt were undermining the Church. Sadly, he was never reconciled to their ideas. In March of the following year Susanna was able to hear more of her sons from George Whitfield, an evangelist who was closely associated with the Wesley brothers. He also was an itinerant preacher and, accompanied by a companion, was travelling through the West Country. They stopped at the Hall's parsonage in Fisherton to visit Susanna who was still not happy about her two younger sons.

"I do not like their way of living," she told them. "I wish they could have some place of their own where they might regularly preach."

"But you cannot conceive of the good they do, Mrs Wesley," said George Whitfield enthusiastically. "Indeed the greatest part of our clergy are asleep and there never was a greater need of itinerant preachers than now."

The other gentleman interrupted. "I was converted through the preaching of your son, Charles. Both your sons spend their time doing good."

Susanna was not convinced and she had another concern. "I fear, Mr Whitfield, my sons plan to make some innovations in the Church."

"I assure you ma'am, they are so far from it that they endeavour to reconcile dissenters to our Communion. Your son John baptised five adult Presbyterians in our own way

---

58   Stevenson, *Memorials of the Welsey Family*

on St Paul's day. He believes that will bring many over to our Communion."

Susanna looked relieved. "I am glad to hear it."

Later Patty was told of the visit. "Mr Whitfield seems a very good man." Susanna told her daughter. "I could not talk with him as much as I desired but he is one who truly desires the salvation of mankind." [59]

John had now established himself in London. He had bought an old Foundery on Windmill Hill. This had been damaged by an explosion some years previously but he raised enough money to rebuild it. As well as a Chapel, there were several rooms and Susanna hoped she might be able to make her home with him. When the Halls moved to London, she went with them and later the same year she moved into the Foundery to spend her last years with John and Charles. Soon afterwards she, too, had a spiritual experience similar to that of her sons.

One warm August day in 1739 she knelt, as she had done so many times before, to receive the bread and the wine. Patty's husband, Westley Hall, was celebrating Communion on that day. As he handed her the cup and pronounced the familiar words, 'The blood of our Lord Jesus Christ which was given for thee', she felt an almost physical pain in her heart and tears filled her eyes. For the first time she understood what John and Charles had been trying to tell her.

"Those words struck at my heart," she told John later. "Suddenly I knew God for Christ's sake had forgiven *me* all *my* sins. Until a short time since, I had scarce heard such a thing mentioned as the having forgiveness of sins now or God's Spirit bearing witness with our spirit." She smiled

---

59   Stevenson, *Memorials of the Wesley Family* (adapted)

warmly at her son. "Much less did I imagine that this was the common privilege of all true believers. But now I know." [60]

"I am glad you, too, know that God has forgiven you your sins because of Christ's sacrifice."

"In my head I always knew it but now I know it in my heart too. I must write to Sammy. Would that he too could know this marvellous experience. I would so like to talk to him of it."

But Susanna was not to see her eldest son again. Early in the morning of 6th November 1739, Sammy died peacefully in his sleep. This was a great sadness for her but she coped with her usual resilience, writing soon afterwards to Charles:

> Your brother was exceedingly dear to me in his life, and perhaps I have erred in loving him too well. I once thought it impossible to bear his loss, but none know what they can bear until they are tried ... I rejoice in having a comfortable hope of my dear son's salvation. He is now at rest and would not return to earth to gain the world. Why then should I mourn? [61]

After Sammy's death, Susanna became very involved in the work of the Foundery and in the Methodist movement as it came to be called. The name had been first used when John and Charles were at Oxford. Neither had intended to form a new 'church'. They wanted the Church of England to return to its roots in the early church. Only ordained Anglican clergymen were permitted to preach and to take services in the Foundery Chapel. Methodism was still part of the Church of England although Methodist services did

---

60   Adapted from *The Journal of John Wesley* for 3rd Sept 1739
61   Stevenson, *Memorials of the Wesley Family*

not always adhere rigidly to all the ritual of the mother Church.

Susanna found her new life stimulating. She gradually became aware that her sons' evangelistic fervour was bringing about the revival of the Christian faith prophesied by her High-Church husband. She listened to their preaching and was warmed by it. On one occasion she heard John preach to thousands of people on Kennington Common and as she did so, she knew that her 'brand plucked from the burning' was lighting fires in the hearts of his listeners that would burn on over the years. She was now convinced that what her sons were doing was of God.

However that did not stop her missing them and wishing John could spend more time with her. She wrote to Charles that his brother's visits

> ... are seldom and short, for which I never blame him, because I know he is well employed, and, blessed be God, hath great success in his ministry. But, my dear Charles, still I want either him or you; for, indeed, in the most literal sense, I am become a little child and want continual succour.

There was nothing childlike about her mind, however. It was still as sharp as ever. Her teaching skills were resurrected and she put them to good use at the Foundery. Drawing together groups of women, she taught them from the Bible, encouraging their Christian faith and witness.

John and Charles were now travelling and preaching all over the country. While they were away, a young man named Thomas Maxfield was left in charge of the meetings in the Foundery. As he was not ordained, he was only allowed to read the Scriptures and explain them; he was not permitted to preach. This frustrated him as he was sure he could do it better than some of the clergymen he heard.

One day, to Susanna's astonishment, he climbed into the pulpit and preached a sermon that she wished her sons could have heard. After the service, he looked sheepish and tried unsuccessfully to evade her. When she cornered him, he blushed and looked down at his feet.

"You preach a powerful sermon, Mr Maxfield," she told him.

He looked up, startled. "Why thank you, Mrs Wesley. But I am afraid your sons will not agree."

Susanna knew he was right. It was not long before John heard about the unprecedented preaching of a layman. He hurried back to the Foundery, his face showing his displeasure. His mother met him.

"What has disturbed you, my son?" she asked gently although she was well aware of the cause of his anger.

"I hear Thomas Maxfield, a *layman,* has turned preacher," he growled.

Susanna nodded. "Yes, he preached. Now Jacky, you know my views and that once I would not have favoured anything of the kind. But take care how you treat that young man. He is as surely called of God to preach as you are."

John stared at her. "But mother, he is not an ordained clergyman."

"I suggest you hear him for yourself, Jacky, and then judge him if you must."

She waited as her son struggled with his ingrained prejudice. But she knew he was fair and she had no doubt of the outcome of his deliberations.

"I will hear him," he said at length.

As John listened to the young man, he knew his mother was right. "He preaches the Lord's word," he told her. "Let him do what seems to him right. Who am I that I should hinder God's word?"

Susanna smiled. She had been sure he would be convinced. And if lay preaching were permitted, the Gospel could be spread faster; the number of ordained clergyman prepared to ride around the country to preach was small. Once again Susanna had shown how adaptable she was.

Emilia's marriage had not been happy and in 1740 she joined her mother at the Foundery. Susanna was delighted to have the support of her eldest daughter in her last two years. The following year she was saddened to hear of the death of Kezzy at Bexley. This daughter was only thirty-two but she had always been frail. It was 10th March 1741 when Charles visited her with the news.

"Yesterday morning," he told her, "Sister Kezzy died in the Lord Jesus. She commended her spirit into the hands of Jesus and fell asleep."

Susanna's life was also now drawing to a close. She was becoming much weaker and was increasingly bedridden. Apart from gout, she had no specific disease that finally took her life. She was worn out by the many hardships she had suffered and by her frequent childbearing. As she lay in her bed, weak but with her mind as active as ever, she looked back over her life. It had been hard but she regretted none of it. She knew that the training of her children had born fruit and she had lived to see the revival of the Christian faith, prophesied by her husband, brought about by the preaching of her son — her 'brand plucked from the burning'.

"I have many years suffered much pain and great bodily infirmities," she told Emilia. "But those very sufferings have, by the blessing of God, been of excellent use, and proved the most proper means of reclaiming me from a vain conversation; ... All my sufferings ... have concurred to promote my spiritual and eternal good." [62]

---

62   John Kirk, *The Mother of the Wesleys,* Jarrold 1868

"You have been good to us, Mama. We owe you much. You must sleep now."

Emilia tiptoed out of the room before her mother could see the tears filling her eyes. She knew the end was near. It was July 1742. Charles had left London for North Wales and she was unable to contact him. But John was in Bristol. Emilia hurriedly wrote him a note telling him that their mother was dying. He returned hurriedly to London to find his mother 'on the borders of eternity.' [63]

She smiled at her favourite son and said weakly, "I now have no desire but to depart and to be with Christ." [64]

On Friday 23rd July 1742 her remaining daughters, Emilia, Sukey, Hetty, Anne and Patty were gathered round her bed. John joined them and gently placed his hand over his mother's frail one. She was trying to say something and he bent his head to hear.

"Children, as soon as I am released, sing a psalm of praise to God." [65]

Hetty stifled a sob and Susanna tried to smile at her as John began to say the words of the Commendatory Prayer:

O Almighty God ... we humbly commend the soul of this thy servant, our dear mother, into thy hands ... most humbly beseeching thee that it may be precious in thy sight.

Susanna closed her eyes and smiled. Soon — very soon — she would meet her Saviour and Lord, Jesus Christ, who had died for her. As John's voice died away, she heard soft voices singing round her bed. Was it the voices of her

---

63   Journal of John Wesley 20th July 1742
64   ibid. 20th July 1742
65   ibid. 23rd July 1742

children she could hear? Or was it the singing of angels? The darkness around her was melting into a soft radiant light; she felt weightless and relaxed; all her cares had floated away. The singing grew louder and the light brighter as Susanna Wesley drifted into eternity.

In his Journal for that day John Wesley wrote:

> Almost an innumerable company of people being gathered together, about five in the afternoon I committed to the earth the body of my mother. It was one of the most solemn assemblies I ever saw, or expect to see, this side of eternity. [66]

---

66 Susanna Wesley was buried on Sunday 1st August 1742 in Bunhill Fields, near the Foundery where she had spent her last days. It was a Dissenters' cemetery where John Bunyan was also buried.

Epilogue

There is no doubt Susanna had a great impact on her children—particularly John, and through him on the Methodist movement. Indeed it was the 'method' she had used with her children that gave the movement its name. John was greatly influenced by her and inherited her logical mind and dedication to duty.

Susanna left no worldly goods but she passed on to her children the patience, steadfastness and sincerity that had always been dominant in her character. Seven of her children survived her. John became the most famous evangelist of the century and the revival his preaching engendered had a profound effect on the history of his country. He lived to the great age of eighty seven and died in 1791. He was buried in the grounds of City Road Chapel which replaced the Foundery.

Charles, who ably supported his brother, is well-known as the author of those beautiful hymns that are often sung today. He died at the age of eighty in 1788 declaring on his deathbed that he had lived and died in the Communion of the Church of England. He was buried in the graveyard of his local parish church in Marylebone. The break of the Methodists with the Church of England did not occur until after the death of both John and Charles, neither of whom would have condoned it.

Emilia continued to live at the Foundery. Her husband had died and left her penniless and John supported her. She lived to seventy nine, dying in 1771. Sukey, too, was supported by John after she left her husband and resisted all pleas to return to him. She died in 1784 aged eighty-nine. Hetty's husband did not mend his ways in spite of Charles' efforts to reform him. In her latter years Hetty became an invalid and Charles was the only one of her family who attended her funeral in 1750. She was only fifty-three when she died.

Anne, unlike her sisters, had a happy marriage. There appears to be no record of when she died. Patty moved to London after her husband deserted her and once again she was supported by her brothers. She was very close to John and his death distressed her greatly. She died four months later in 1791 at the age of eighty five.

Intelligent, adaptable and always faithful to her beliefs, Susanna Wesley might have been forgotten had it not been for her sons. But she deserves a place in history for herself. While accepting the eighteenth century relationship between men and women, she was never afraid to stand up for what she believed to be right. Her 'kitchen preaching' was only one example showing how far ahead of her age was the lady who came to be known as the 'Mother of Methodism'.

Bibliography

Brailesford, Mable R., *Susanna Wesley, The Mother of Methodism,* Epworth Press 1938

Clarke, Adam, *Memoirs of the Wesley Family*, 1836

Clarke, Eliza, *Susanna Wesley,* Eminent Women Series 1876

Dallimore, Arnold A., *Susanna Wesley - the Mother of John and Charles Wesley,* Baker Books 1993

Dengler, Sandy, *Susanna Wesley – Servant of God* Moody Press, Chicago 1987

Greetham, Mary, *Susanna Wesley, Mother of Methodism*, (Foundery Press)

Harmon, Rebecca Larmar, *Susanna – Mother of the Wesleys*, Hodder and Stoughton 1968

Harrison, Elsey, G., *Son to Susanna – The Private Life of John Wesley*

Headingley MSS, *Susanna's Prayers and Meditations*, Wesley College, Bristol

Kirk, John, *The Mother of the Wesleys,* 1867

Maser, Frederick E., *The Wesley Sisters*, Foundery Press

Bibliography

Newton, John A., *Susanna Wesley and the Puritan Tradition in Methodism,* Epworth Press 1968

Snowden, Rita, *Such a Woman: The Story of Susanna Wesley*, The Upper Room, Nashville, 1962

Stevenson, George J., *Memorials of the Wesley Family*, Partridge 1876

Tyerman, Luke, *Life and Times of John Wesley* 1871

Tyerman, Luke, *Life and Times of Samuel Wesley* 1866

Quiller-Couch, Sir Arthur, *Hetty Wesley*, J M Dent & Sons Ltd 1903

Wesley, John, *The Journal of John Wesley* Abridged by Christopher Idle, Lion 1986

Index

1) Members of the Wesley and Annesley Families

Annesley, Dr Samuel
   (Susanna's father)
   Biographical note . . 11f (n.)
   Influence on daughter 12ff
   Death 42

Annesley, Elizabeth
   Married Dunton, John 17f
   Death 50

Annesley, Judith 21f

Annesley, Samuel
   (Susanna's brother)
   His fortune 128ff
   Disappearance . . . 137f, 140-8

Wesley, Anne, (Nancy)
   Birth 71
   Married Lambert, J. . 167
   Death (no record) . . 211

Wesley, Charles,
   Birth 81

Education 141-5, 172
Death 210

Wesley, Emilia
Birth 34
Character 43, 47, 53-6, 76, 92f,
. . . . 135f, 193, 195, 207f
Teacher 132, 171f, 185, 196
Love and marriage . 131, 197f
Death 211

Wesley, Hetty see Mehetabel

Wesley, John (Jacky)
Birth 71
Education 72, 131, 172
Conversion 201
Fire rescue 86
Preaching 201ff
Visit to U.S.A. . . . 198ff
Death 210

Wesley, Kezzy
Birth 90
Character 97, 199f
Love 198f
Death 211

Wesley, Martha (Patty)
Birth 81
Love and marriage . 189ff
Death 211

Wesley, Mary (Molly)
Birth 37
Character 37f, 187
Marries Whitelamb, J. 187
Moves to Wroot . . . 188f
Death 189

Wesley, Matthew
   (Susanna's brother-in-law)
   Visits 88, 128, 140-8, 181ff
   Criticises
   Samuel Wesley . . . 184f
Wesley, Samuel (Sammy junior)
   Birth 30f
   Education 36f, 52, 58f, 72, 92, 110, 136f
   Marriage 111
   Death 210
Wesley, Samuel (senior)
   Marriage 27
   Character and
   theology 19f, 23-6, 38- 41, 45
   Writings 26, 63
   Rector 49f, 72f
   Farming 51
   Finances 38, 44
   Accidents 175f, 179ff
   Death 192f
Wesley, Susanna (Sukey)
   (Daughter of Susanna & Samuel)
   Birth 34
   Letters 91f
   Love 128-131
   Death 211
Wesley, Ursula, ... 111, 138ff
   (wife of Sammy Wesley)

Index

2) *Other people*

Anne, Queen of England 65

Attkins, Will 152-60

Bathurst, Elizabeth . . . 16

Buckingham, Duke of . 110

Castleton, Lord . . . . (see Normanby)

Charles II . . . . 12n.

Dunton, John 17ff, 27

Ellison, Richard 130f, 150f

Hall, Westley 189-91, 200, 203

Harper, Robert 197f

Hoole, Rev. Joseph . . . 120, 122f, 167, 180

Inman, Rev. John 100f, 108f

Lambert, John 167

Leybourne, Robert . . . 131, 198

Marshall (nanny) 111

Mary, Queen of England 25, 41, 65

Massey, Betty (maid) . 53ff, 75, 111

Normanby, Marquis of . 31ff, 39ff, 63

Potter, John
    Bishop of Oxford . . 167, 178

Romley, John 150f, 157-60

Sharpe, Archbishop of
    York 78ff

Taylor, Mrs 172, 183

Whitelamb, Johnny . . . 132, 177, 187ff

William III, of Orange . 25f, 64

Whitfield, George . . . 202

Wright, William 135, 158f, 153-7

Yarborough, Lady . . . 65f

3) Index of Names of Places and Institutions

All Hallows the Wall . . 17

Bunhills Fields . . . . . 209n.

Charterhouse 110, 131

East India Company . . 146

Epwort 41, 43, 173, 178, 187

Gainsborough 160, 181, 203-7

Haxey 120, 167, 180

Kelstern 151

Lincoln
   Town 132, 135, 171, 185
   Castle 77
   Cathedral 157f

Little St Helens 15

London 15, 63, 138-48, 170

Louth 167f

Oxford 139, 172-8, 188
   Lincoln College, . . 172, 188

St Giles . . . . 12n.

South Ormsby 31-4, 43

Wesminster School . . . 72, 91, 110

Wroot 167, 178, 187-9

Shut Up Sarah
by
Marion Field

W as she privileged? Sarah was born into the Taylorites, the most exclusive of those Brethren who look to J N Darby as founder. You may have seen them:

- Women with scarves who stick together
- Schoolchildren who never accept invitations
- Groups of men declaiming the Bible on the street

This true story of a teenage daughter refusing to be browbeaten by either family or elders will be compulsive reading for mature teenagers struggling between loyalty and the need of change—as well as for any who want to understand how certain Brethren could have lost their way.

'I highly recommend this book ... This gifted writer in her second book has written a true story in a compelling fictional style.'
Jennifer Rees-Larcombe

ISBN 1-897913-28-1

Highland Books   Price £5.99

A Window To Heaven

Dr Diane M. Komp

W hat would you do as a hospital doctor when children facing death—or their parents—witness to you about faith? The official line is not to get involved, to stay 'professional'. But that was not Dr Komp's reaction …

'I have met people who claim they lost their faith over the agonising question, How can a loving God let innocent children die? Dr Komp is the first person I've met who found a personal faith while treating such dying children. Her story —and theirs— deserves our attention'.
Philip Yancey
Author of *Disappointment with God*

'Unforgettably inspiring'
Sandy Millar, Holy Trinity Brompton

'Out of harrowing experiences while looking after children with cancer, Diane Komp, a paediatric oncologist of international repute, draws conclusions about the human condition that should make us pause and think …
I read it with a lump in my throat.'
J.S. Malpas D.Phil., FRCP, FRCR, FFPM
St Bartholomew's Hospital, London
ISBN 1-897913-32-X
Highland Books   Price £3.99

Don't Call Me Sister

Marion Field

In this award-winning book, Marion Field at last releases the pent-up anger, fear and frustration which has beset her for years. Trapped for years in an absurdly over-the-top strict Brethren sect, she managed finally to confront reality and break free.

This is her own story: perhaps surprisingly for one who suffered the trauma and indignity of trying to squeeze herself into the mould expected of her, it is written with humour, sensitivity and, above all, a generous dose of grace.

'An absorbing, different and very refreshing book.
I can highly recommend it'
Jennifer Rees Larcombe

'Told with honesty and humour'
Eileen Ryder   The Woman Journalist

'Compelling reading. A timely reminder of the
perils of dictatorial leadership'
Alpha Magazine

ISBN 1 897913 45 1

Highland Books   Price £6.99

PLATES

An English family at tea   by Joseph van Aken

The old Annesley House in Spital Yard, London, in which Susanna grew up.

Below, detail of plaque.

IN THIS HOUSE
SUSANNA ANNESLEY
MOTHER OF
JOHN WESLEY
WAS BORN
JANUARY 20TH 1669

IN THE
BUNHILL FIELDS
BURIAL GROUND OPPOSITE
LIE THE REMAINS OF
SUSANNAH WESLEY,
WIDOW OF
THE REV. SAMUEL WESLEY M.A.
RECTOR OF EPWORTH LINCOLNSHIRE
WHO DIED JULY 23rd 1762
AGED 73 YEARS
SHE WAS THE YOUNGEST DAUGHTER OF
THE REV. SAMUEL ANNESLEY D.D.
EJECTED BY THE ACT OF UNIFORMITY
FROM THE RECTORY OF
ST. GILES CRIPPLEGATE AUG. 24th 1662
SHE WAS THE MOTHER OF
THE REVS. JOHN AND CHARLES WESLEY
THE FORMER OF WHOM WAS UNDER GOD
THE FOUNDER OF
THE SOCIETIES OF THE PEOPLE
CALLED METHODISTS

Above: portrait of Susanna as a young woman. *Reproduced by permission of the Trustees for Methodist Purposes.*

Above left: A funerary monument in the grounds of Wesley's Chapel, City Road. *Reproduced by permission of the Trustees of the Wesley Chapel.*

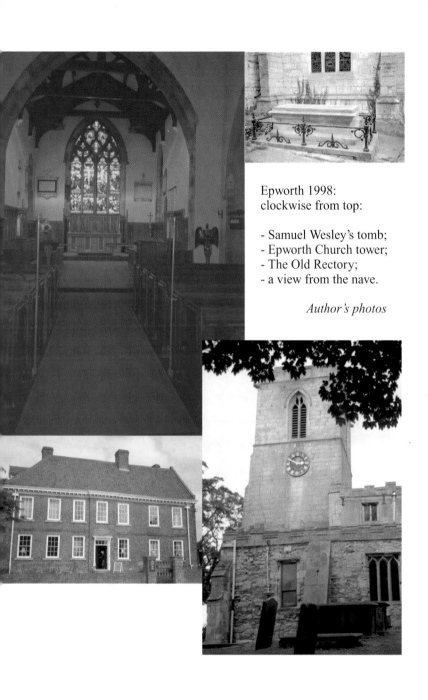

Epworth 1998:
clockwise from top:

- Samuel Wesley's tomb;
- Epworth Church tower;
- The Old Rectory;
- a view from the nave.

Author's photos

Letter to John Wesley in the hand of Susanna, first part

Reproduced with permission of the Trustees of Wesley's Chapel.

Letter to John Wesley, continued from previous page
Reproduced with permission of the Trustees of Wesley's Chapel.

Left: statue of John Wesley, outside Wesley's Chapel, City Road, London, (inscription: 'The World is my parish') not far from the site of 'The Foundery' (plaque, below left), where Susanna spent her last years.

By permission of the Trustees of Wesley's Chapel.

Below, the *Aldersgate Flame,* a modern sculpture recording John Welsey's conversion experience (detail at bottom).

THE WORLD IS MY PARISH

FORTY YARDS SOUTH OF THIS BUILDING
ON THE EAST MOUND WAS THE SITE OF
THE FOUNDERY
JOHN WESLEY'S HEADQUARTERS 1739-78
AND THE FIRST METHODIST BOOK-ROOM
THE MOTHER OF THE WESLEYS DIED THERE
30TH JULY 1742
ERECTED BY THE BRITISH SECTION OF
THE INTERNATIONAL METHODIST HISTORICAL UNION
24TH MAY 1932

I felt my Heart ſtrangely warm'd.

JOHN WESLEY.

A view of Lincoln Castle, which gives some idea of a 17th-Century prisoner's view of the City.

Right: Susanna's 'prayer chair' on display at Epworth, showing hinged back and drawer *(see pages 61 and 195).*

Author's photo reproduced by permission of the Trustees of Epworth Old Rectory.

The Happy Marriage VI:
the country dance

William Hogarth   c. 1745